TECHNICAL
REPORT

The Effect of Military Enlistment on Earnings and Education

David S. Loughran, Paco Martorell,
Trey Miller, Jacob Alex Klerman

Prepared for the United States Army

Approved for public release; distribution unlimited

RAND ARROYO CENTER

The research described in this report was sponsored by the United States Army under Contract No. W74V8H-06-C-0001.

Library of Congress Cataloging-in-Publication Data

The effect of military enlistment on earnings and education / David S. Loughran ... [et al.].
p. cm.
Includes bibliographical references.
ISBN 978-0-8330-5823-2 (pbk. : alk. paper)
1. Veterans—United States—Economic conditions. 2. Veterans—Education—United States—Statistics. 3. Educational attainment—United States—Statistics. 4. Income—United States—Statistics. I. Loughran, David S., 1969-

UB357.E37 2011
331.2'97308697—dc23

20110343692

The RAND Corporation is a nonprofit institution that helps improve policy and decisionmaking through research and analysis. RAND's publications do not necessarily reflect the opinions of its research clients and sponsors.

RAND® is a registered trademark.

Published 2011 by the RAND Corporation
1776 Main Street, P.O. Box 2138, Santa Monica, CA 90407-2138
1200 South Hayes Street, Arlington, VA 22202-5050
4570 Fifth Avenue, Suite 600, Pittsburgh, PA 15213-2665
RAND URL: http://www.rand.org/
To order RAND documents or to obtain additional information, contact
Distribution Services: Telephone: (310) 451-7002;
Fax: (310) 451-6915; Email: order@rand.org

Preface

Each year, more than 150,000 young men and women enlist in the active component of the U.S. military. The experience of these enlistees while serving their country will undoubtedly influence their long-run labor market outcomes, but just how is not well understood. The research described in this report seeks to estimate the causal effect of military enlistment on labor market earnings and educational attainment as many as 18 years following enlistment. The report will be of interest to policymakers and military manpower analysts interested in how early military experiences affect long-run labor market and educational outcomes.

This research was sponsored by the United States Army Accessions Command and conducted within RAND Arroyo Center's Manpower and Training Program. RAND Arroyo Center, part of the RAND Corporation, is a federally funded research and development center sponsored by the United States Army.

The Project Unique Identification Code (PUIC) for the project that produced this document is RAND10469.

For more information on RAND Arroyo Center, contact the Director of Operations (telephone 310-393-0411, extension 6419; FAX 310-451-6952; email Marcy_Agmon@rand.org) or visit the Arroyo Center's website at http://www.rand.org/ard/.

Contents

Figures

Tables

Summary

Military compensation is one of the Department of Defense's most important means for attracting and retaining a force of young men and women qualified to meet the nation's national security objectives. As such, it is natural to want to compare military compensation with the compensation service members might receive were they to work in the civilian economy instead. Interpreting the difference in earnings between veterans and nonveterans, though, is complicated by the fact that individuals who do and do not serve in the military differ in ways that are likely to influence their earnings. The selective nature of military service makes it difficult to determine whether the observed difference in earnings is attributable to military service or to differences in the characteristics of these individuals.

In the research reported here, we refine comparisons between the earnings of enlistees and non-enlistees employing an approach first implemented by Angrist (1998). The core assumption we make is that an enlistee drawn at random from the pool of military applicants will be more similar to a randomly selected applicant that did not enlist than to a randomly selected non-applicant. Thus, we assume that differences in the earnings of military applicants who do and do not ultimately enlist will provide a better estimate of the causal effect of enlistment than will differences in the earnings of enlistees and all non-enlistees combined (i.e., non-enlisted applicants and non-applicants). We further assume that the rich set of applicant characteristics recorded on the military application record, information that is not found in the typical survey, controls adequately for any remaining differences between applicants who do and do not enlist that are correlated with earnings. Although this assumption, which Angrist refers to as the assumption of "selection on observables," is quite strong, it is perhaps not unreasonable in this particular context, in which the sample is restricted to individuals with a common propensity to apply for military service and the available control variables are those that the military uses to screen applicants for service.

Our analysis expands on the work of Angrist (1998) in several important ways. First, we employ data on more recent cohorts of military applicants (individuals applying for military service between 1989 and 2003). Second, we follow military applicants for as many as 18 years following application, allowing us to estimate longer-run effects of enlistment on earnings. Third, our estimates account for military allowances and bonuses, which constitute a significant portion of military earnings. Fourth, our estimates are conditioned on a broader range of observable differences between enlistees and non-enlistees, including earnings prior to application. Finally, our analyses consider not only how enlistment affects earnings, but also how it affects a critical determinant of earnings, college education.

Data and Methods

We employ administrative data on military applicants applying for active-component enlisted service between 1989 and 2003. We restrict our sample to the typical qualified applicant: individuals 17 and older with at most a high school diploma (excluding those with varying levels of postsecondary education) who meet the military's minimum enlistment standards with respect to aptitude, health, and drug and alcohol use. We obtained longitudinal earnings data for each of these applicants from military pay files and the Social Security Administration. Our measure of earnings captures virtually all cash compensation paid to these individuals from military and civilian sources. Data on college enrollment and degree attainment for a subsample of applicants were obtained from the National Student Clearinghouse, a nonprofit organization that contracts with institutions of higher education to verify college enrollment and degree receipt for student loan agencies. The earnings data span 1994 to 2007, and the college enrollment and degree attainment data span 1991 to 2010.

With these individual-level longitudinal administrative data, we estimate the effect of enlistment on earnings and education by years since application, controlling for age, gender, year of application, service, race/ethnicity, educational attainment, and scores on the Armed Forces Qualification Test (AFQT). Our earnings model also controls for earnings prior to application.

Although we believe these data allow for better estimates of the effect of enlistment on earnings and education than are typically found in the literature, we acknowledge several limitations with our approach. First, it could be that we do not fully control for differences between enlistees and non-enlistees that are correlated with earnings and education. As such, our estimates could still be biased estimates of the true causal effect of enlistment on earnings and education. Second, we estimate the effect of ever having enlisted rather than the effect of a specific length of military service. Although we observe years of military service in our data, it is less plausible that the covariates available on the applicant record are sufficient to control for differences in enlistees who serve for different periods of time; therefore, comparing the educational attainment or earnings of such persons would confound the potential effects of individual differences on outcomes with those of military service. Third, we estimate the effect of enlistment on cash compensation rather than on total compensation, which would include the value of health, deferred, and in-kind benefits. While we know exactly what those benefits are in the military context, assigning a cash-equivalent value to them can be difficult. Furthermore, while we can directly observe the cash compensation of applicants that do not enlist, we do not observe their noncash benefits. Making the necessary imputations for all of our 15 applicant cohorts is beyond the scope of this study.

Results

Figure S.1 graphs the average estimated effect of Army enlistment on annual earnings for individuals applying for active-component service between 1989 and 2003. Figure S.2 graphs these effects as a percentage of non-enlistee earnings. In both figures, data points above the horizontal line at zero indicate a positive effect of enlistment on earnings, and points below that line indicate a negative effect of enlistment on earnings. The dashed lines denote the estimated 95 percent confidence interval surrounding these estimates.

Figure S.1
Estimated Effect of Army Enlistment on Annual Earnings ($2005), by Years Since Application

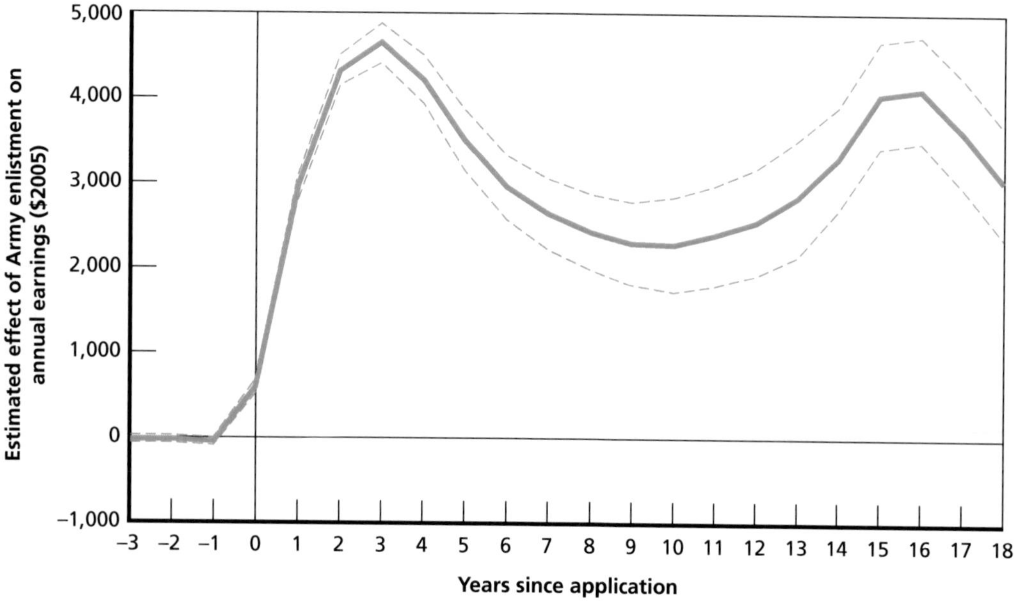

NOTES: Sample restricted to Army applicants. Dashed lines denote 95 percent confidence intervals.
RAND *TR995-S.1*

Figure S.2
Estimated Percentage Effect of Army Enlistment on Annual Earnings, by Years Since Application

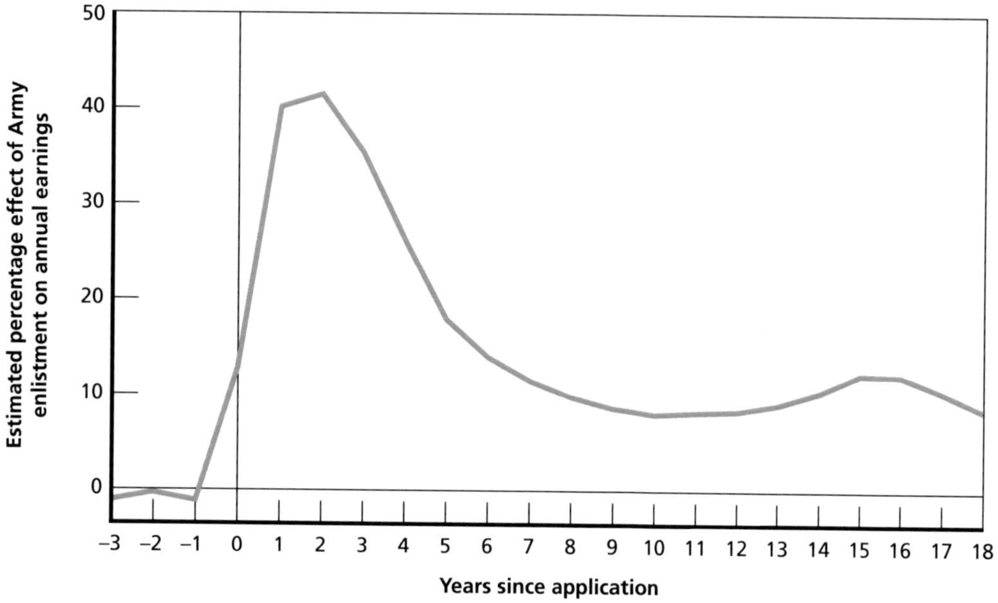

NOTES: Sample restricted to Army applicants. Percentages are computed relative to the earnings of non-enlistees.
RAND *TR995-S.2*

Since we control for differences in pre-application earnings, applicants who do and do not enlist have nearly identical earnings prior to the year of application. In the first three to four years following application (years 0–3), the figures show a strong positive effect of Army enlistment on earnings. The positive estimated effect of enlistment peaks two years following application, at 42 percent, and then declines through the 10th year following application.

Differences in the timing of postsecondary education between enlistees and non-enlistees likely account for some of the pattern in earnings effects we observe. In the years immediately following application, enlistees are working full-time in an occupation that pays relatively well for someone with only a high school education. Had these individuals not enlisted, some fraction of them would have attended college instead and, as a result, would likely have been working less than full-time, consequently earning comparatively little. By three years following the year of application, however, a large fraction of enlistees will have separated from the active component.[1] Many of these individuals will attend college when they separate and presumably work relatively little in those years. Meanwhile, had these individuals never enlisted, they would be further along in their schooling or their civilian careers at this juncture.

Differences in civilian employment and work experience are also likely to contribute to the pattern of estimated earnings effects. Military employment offers stable full-time work, whereas the civilian jobs individuals typically hold in the first few years after high school are characterized by high turnover. Between four and eight years following application, when enlistees are separating from the military in large numbers, those that do not go to college enter civilian jobs with less civilian work experience than they otherwise would have, which could lead to lower earnings, all else equal.

The estimates presented in Figures S.1 and S.2 indicate that the positive effect of Army enlistment on earnings persists in the longer run. By 14–18 years following application, our estimates imply that Army enlistment increases annual earnings, on average, by 11 percent.

Figure S.3 shows that these estimated earnings effects are considerably stronger for individuals scoring between the 31st and 50th percentiles of the AFQT distribution (Category IIIB). We also find, conditional on AFQT, that enlistment increases the earnings of African Americans and Hispanics substantially more than it does for whites. We find little difference between men and women in the impact of Army enlistment on earnings.

Our college enrollment and degree attainment estimates clearly indicate that Army enlistment delays college education, but our relatively small sample for the Army makes it impossible to draw firm conclusions about the longer-run effect of Army enlistment on educational attainment (see the wide confidence intervals surrounding the two- and four-year college degree attainment estimates in Figure S.4 in year 18). However, when we examine a larger sample covering all services combined (see Figure S.5), our estimates indicate a small positive longer-run effect of enlistment on two-year college degree attainment and a small negative effect of enlistment on four-year college degree attainment. The college degree attainment estimates for all services combined are statistically indistinguishable from those for the Army alone.

---

[1] Year 3 after the application year corresponds to the fourth year of service in our analysis, since year 0 is the year of application.

Figure S.3
Estimated Percentage Effect of Army Enlistment on Annual Earnings, by Years Since Application and AFQT Category

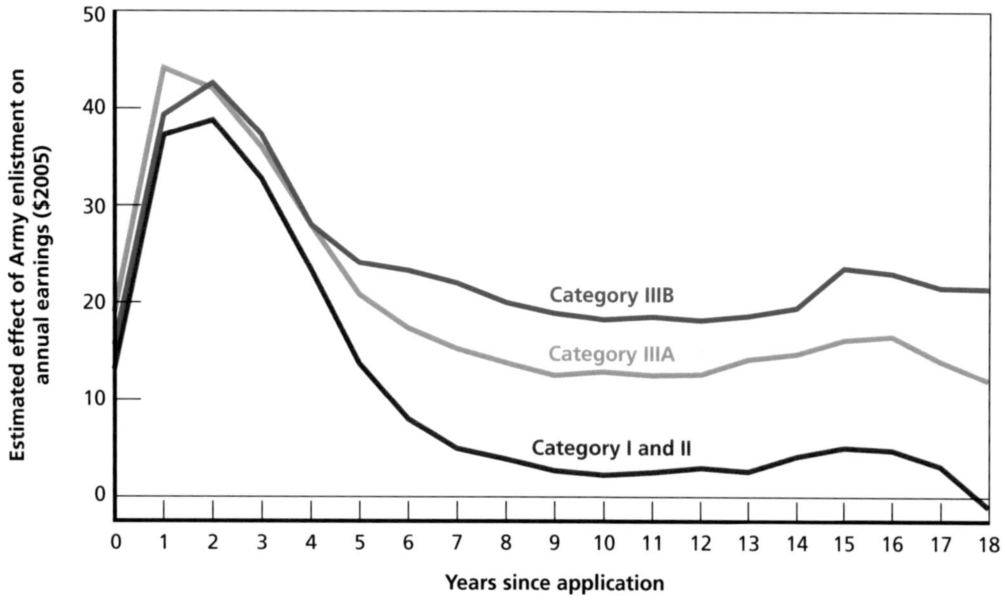

NOTE: Sample restricted to Army applicants.
RAND *TR995-S.3*

Figure S.4
Estimated Effect of Army Enlistment on College Degree Attainment, by Years Since Application

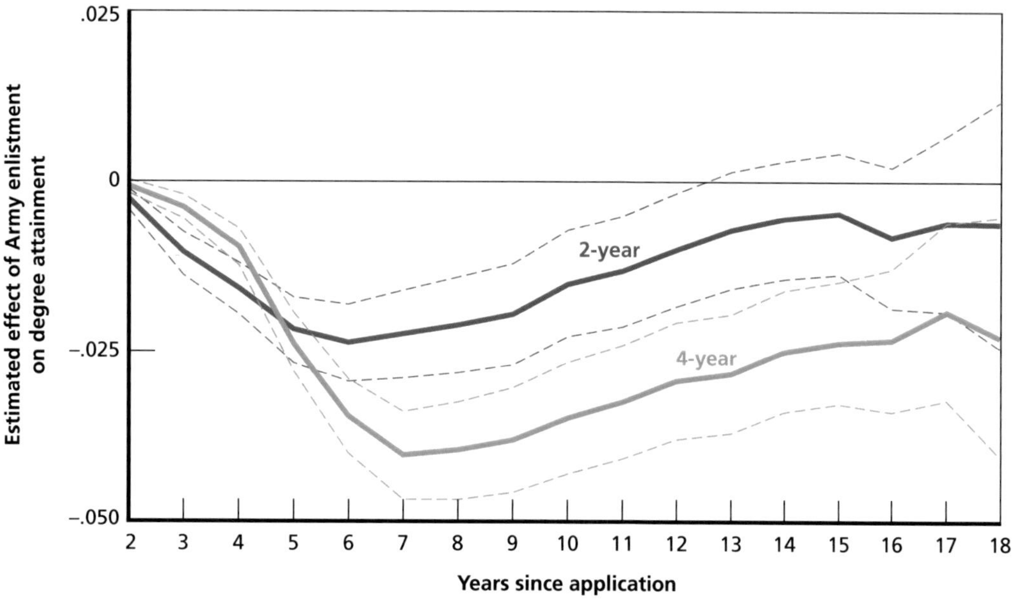

NOTES: Sample restricted to 1991–1994 Army applicant cohorts. Dashed lines denote 95 percent confidence intervals.
RAND *TR995-S.4*

Figure S.5
Estimated Effect of Enlistment on College Degree Attainment, by Years Since Application: All Services Combined

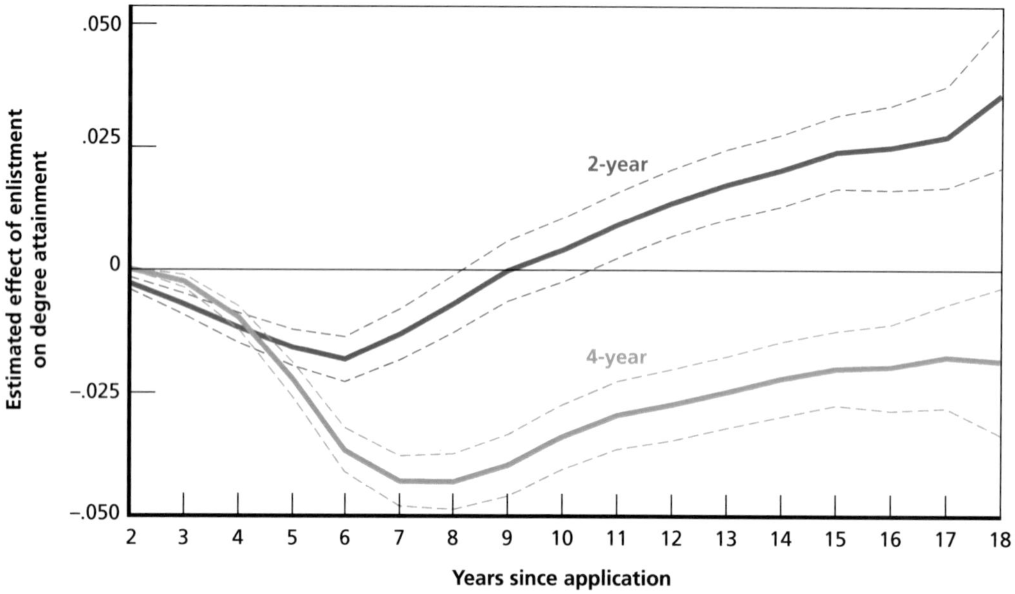

NOTES: Sample restricted to 1991–1994 applicant cohorts. Dashed lines denote 95 percent confidence intervals.
RAND *TR995-S.5*

Discussion

A strong, positive, short-run effect of enlistment on earnings is perhaps unsurprising, since the alternative to military service for many young men and women is college rather than full-time work. In addition, it could very well be that the military must offer a relatively high wage in order to induce individuals to choose enlistment and the risks and hardships it entails. That enlistment might convey longer-run benefits in the labor market is perhaps of greater significance for military manpower policy.

There are at least three potential explanations for these longer-run, positive earnings effects. First, it could be that enlistment induces enlistees to obtain more formal education than they otherwise would have obtained and that this greater educational attainment has returns in the labor market. We find, at best, weak evidence in support of this hypothesis. On the one hand, our estimates clearly indicate that enlistment causes enlistees to delay their college education. All else equal, we might expect such a delay to depress longer-run labor market earnings. However, our estimates also indicate that enlistment increases the likelihood that enlistees will obtain a two-year college degree, although these estimates are statistically significant only when looking at all services combined. The increase in two-year degree attainment does not emerge until 16–18 years following enlistment, and the value of obtaining such a degree at that age might be much less than at some earlier age. Moreover, for AFQT Category I and II enlistees, the evidence suggests that the increase in two-year degree attainment comes at the expense of four-year degree attainment. The overall effect of enlistment on two-year college degree attainment is small in both absolute and relative terms, suggesting that it is unlikely that these education effects could account for the substantial longer-run earnings effects we estimate.

If enlistment does not have a strong effect on educational attainment, then what explains the longer-run earnings effects we observe? Two possibilities are that (1) military service develops other skills that are valued in the labor market and (2) the military pays above-average wages in order to compensate individuals for their sacrifice and service (a "compensating wage differential"). We do not directly test these alternative hypotheses, but we do find that the positive effect of enlistment on longer-run earnings is concentrated among enlistees who are still serving in the military. The earnings of Category IIIA and IIIB Army enlistees still serving in the military between 14 and 18 years following enlistment are 125 and 155 percent higher, respectively, than the earnings of comparable non-enlistees. By contrast, Category IIIA and IIIB Army enlistees who have separated by 14–18 years following enlistment earn 3 and 6 percent more than comparable non-enlistees, respectively. Category I and II Army enlistees still serving at that juncture earn 84 percent more than comparable non-enlistees, but those enlistees who have separated earn 6 percent less.

The magnitude of the differences in earnings estimates between enlistees who do and do not continue to serve in later years suggests that some of the longer-run earnings effects are attributable to a compensating wage differential. For Category I and II enlistees, it seems likely that this differential explains all of the positive longer-run earnings gains observed for that group as a whole, since the correlation between enlistment and earnings of those who have separated from active-component service is actually negative and our estimates further suggest that enlistment could cause Category I and II enlistees to obtain less formal education than they otherwise would have. Category IIIA and IIIB enlistees, on the other hand, appear to benefit from enlistment even after they separate, although their earnings gains are fairly modest. This suggests that military service may, in fact, help at least some individuals develop skills that convey longer-run benefits in the civilian labor market.

In the All-Volunteer era, the overriding objective of compensation policy is to attract and retain the force necessary to meet the nation's national security objectives. If individuals believe they will be well served by this experience, more might be willing to enlist. Furthermore, from a societal perspective, the electorate might be more willing to support putting young men and women at risk for the sake of national defense if it believes these individuals will benefit financially. The estimates reported in this document suggest that, for the bulk of the enlisted force, military service provides tangible benefits in terms of longer-term earnings. On average, these individuals will earn more and obtain as much, or more, formal education as they otherwise would have. The evidence for the highest-aptitude youth is mixed. Clearly, in the short run, these individuals experience substantial earnings gains as a result of military service. However, those earnings gains erode over time and, for those who do not remain in the military, eventually turn slightly negative, perhaps because enlistment delays college and permanently lowers the likelihood they will obtain a four-year college degree.

Acknowledgments

This research would not have been possible without the assistance of dedicated staff within the United States Army Accessions Command (USAAC), Office of the Secretary of Defense (OSD), Social Security Administration (SSA), and the National Student Clearinghouse (NSC). We are especially thankful to LTC Douglas Gilbert, LTC Gregory Lamm, and COL Jeffrey Schamburg working within USAAC for their guidance and support throughout the project. We are indebted to Michael Risha of SSA, Jeff Tanner and Diana Gillum of NSC, and Richard Moreno, Kathleen Moreno, and Marisa Michaels of the Defense Manpower Data Center (DMDC) for assisting us with obtaining and interpreting the data employed in this research. We thank our RAND colleagues Bruce Orvis, Michael Hansen, and Paul Heaton and John Warner of Clemson University for their careful reviews of this document and many helpful suggestions. Finally, we thank Craig Martin and Alessandro Malchiodi of RAND for providing excellent programming support.

Abbreviations

AFQT	Armed Forces Qualification Test
ASVAB	Armed Services Vocational Aptitude Battery
BAH	Basic Allowance for Housing
BAS	Basic Allowance for Subsistence
DMDC	Defense Manpower Data Center
DoD	U.S. Department of Defense
FICA	Federal Insurance Contribution Act
FSA	Family Separation Allowance
MEPCOM	Military Entrance Processing Command
MEF	Master Earnings File
NSC	National Student Clearinghouse
OSD	Office of the Secretary of Defense
SSA	Social Security Administration
USAAC	U.S. Army Accessions Command

CHAPTER ONE

Introduction

In FY2009, 161,588 young men and women enlisted in the active component of the U.S. military (OUSD P&R, 2010, Table B-1). Based on historical statistics, about half of these enlistees will separate from the active component within four years and more than 80 percent will separate within eight years.[1] Upon leaving the active component, most enlistees will be entering the civilian labor market in earnest for the first time, and it is an open question just how well their military experience and training will serve them in their civilian careers.[2]

Military service is likely to benefit the labor market outcomes of enlistees in a variety of ways. For an enlistee just finishing high school, the military provides a steady, full-time job at above average wages,[3] facilitating the accumulation of work experience and vocational training that civilian employers value. In addition to fostering the development of specific technical skills, the military environment is conducive to the development of certain "soft" skills, such as discipline, punctuality, and self-confidence (Furstenberg, 2005).[4] Many enlistees accumulate funding for postsecondary education through the Montgomery GI Bill, Army College Fund, and other programs that they can use to obtain additional vocational training or attend a two- or four-year college either while they serve or after they separate from the active component, which in turn could lead to improved labor market outcomes. These educational benefits could be particularly valuable to lower-aptitude youth who do not qualify for merit-based scholarships and cannot afford tuition and living expenses, even with need-based financial aid (Krueger, 2004).

While enlistees may, in fact, experience all of these benefits of military service, the central question we seek to address in the research reported in this document is whether enlistees ultimately have higher labor market earnings than they otherwise would have. That is, had an enlistee not enlisted, would he or she have developed fewer skills, obtained less education, and worked in a less stable, lower-paying job? Or, conversely, would entering school or beginning a civilian career upon graduating from high school have ultimately resulted in higher lifetime labor market earnings? Military work experience is not necessarily equivalent to civilian work experience. Grissmer (1992), for example, finds that only one-quarter to one-half of specific military occupations have direct counterparts in the civilian sector, suggesting that military

[1] See Chapter Two for description of data used to generate these statistics.

[2] This report addresses the effect of non-prior-service active-component military service on the enlisted force. We do not consider officers or individuals whose initial military service was in the reserve components.

[3] See, for example, Asch, Hosek, and Martin (2002) and OUSD P&R (2008).

[4] More generally, see, for example, Kelty, Kleykamp, and Segal (2010) and Symonds, Schwartz, and Ferguson (2011) for research on how military service supports youth development and the transition to adulthood.

experience may be a poor substitute for civilian experience in many cases.[5] Moreover, enlistees have lower civilian firm-specific tenure than they would have otherwise, which could further depress their civilian labor market earnings. Finally, while many enlistees obtain formal education while serving, it is likely that they will complete that education later than they would have had they not enlisted, meaning that any labor market return to that educational attainment will be enjoyed for fewer years.

A long line of empirical research has sought to determine whether enlistment during the All-Volunteer era (1973 and later) has a causal impact on labor market earnings.[6] Much of that literature employs survey data to compare the labor market earnings of enlisted veterans and nonveterans, controlling for standard demographic characteristics of survey respondents, such as age, gender, race/ethnicity, and educational attainment. This literature typically finds that enlistees earn more than non-enlistees (Bryant, Samaranayake, and Wilhite, 1993; Magnum and Ball, 1989; Phillips et al., 1992; Andrisani and Daymont, 1998; Stafford, 1991).

However, it is unclear whether these past studies adequately control for differences between individuals who do and do not enlist in the military that are themselves correlated with labor market earnings (hereafter referred to as simply "earnings").[7] As such, these estimates cannot necessarily be interpreted as the causal effect of enlistment on earnings (i.e., the effect of enlistment rather than the effect of the characteristics of enlistees). For example, even conditional on age, race/ethnicity, and education, the average enlistee might be healthier and otherwise more skilled than the average non-enlistee. Such differences could translate into differences in earnings that, in the absence of appropriate controls, would be interpreted as differences attributable to enlistment. And even with rich survey data that allow one to control for such observable differences between enlistees and non-enlistees, there are likely to be other differences between enlistees and non-enlistees—for example, in attitudes toward risk and authority—for which the researcher cannot control.

In the research reported here, we refine comparisons between the earnings of enlistees and non-enlistees employing an approach first implemented by Angrist (1998). Angrist assumes that an enlistee drawn at random from the pool of military applicants will be more similar to a randomly selected applicant that did not enlist than to a randomly selected non-applicant. Thus, differences in the earnings of military applicants who do and do not ultimately enlist will provide a better estimate of the causal effect of enlistment than will differences in the earnings of enlistees and all non-enlistees combined (i.e., non-enlisted applicants and non-applicants). Angrist further assumes that the rich set of applicant characteristics recorded on the military application record—information that is not found in the typical survey—controls

[5] Technological advances over the past two decades may have caused military and civilian occupations to become more similar in their requirements than suggested by Grissmer (1992). Goldberg and Warner (1987) find that the association between military service and earnings is strongly related to military occupation.

[6] A number of papers address the effect of involuntary military service on earnings. In a seminal paper, Angrist (1990) estimates the effect of conscription during the Vietnam War on earnings by exploiting the nearly random variation in military enlistment induced by the draft lottery system in place at that time. Employing this method, Angrist (1990) finds that Vietnam-era veterans suffered large (15 percent) earnings losses. Angrist and Chen (2007), however, find that these earnings losses are close to zero 30 years following conscription. Angrist and Krueger (1994) find smaller negative effects of conscription on the earnings of veterans of World War II and the Korean War.

[7] Hirsch and Mehay (2003) find that active-component service has no effect on the earnings of enlisted members of the reserve components (Reserve and National Guard). By focusing on reservists, the study controls for selection into military service, but it is not clear whether the resulting estimates generalize to nonreservists.

adequately for any remaining differences between applicants who do and do not enlist that are correlated with earnings. Although this assumption, which Angrist refers to as the assumption of "selection on observables," is quite strong, it is perhaps not unreasonable in this particular context, in which the sample is restricted to individuals with a common propensity to apply for military service and the available control variables are those that the military uses to screen applicants for service.

Using data for individuals applying for military service between 1979 and 1982, Angrist (1998) reports that enlistment increases earnings substantially in the first three years following application. That earnings difference, however, diminishes and turns negative in subsequent years. By the end of his data, 12 years following application, the Angrist estimates show a modest (about 10 percent) positive effect of enlistment on the earnings of African American enlistees and no effect on the earnings of white enlistees.

Although we employ an empirical model similar to that of Angrist (1998), our overall approach differs in several important ways. First, our estimates apply to more recent cohorts of military applicants (individuals applying for military service between 1989 and 2003). Second, we follow military applicants for more years, as many as 18 years following application, allowing us to estimate longer-run effects of enlistment. Third, our estimates account for military allowances and bonuses, which constitute a significant portion of military earnings. Fourth, our estimates are conditioned on a broader range of observable differences between enlistees and non-enlistees, including earnings prior to application.

As we report below, our estimates imply that enlistment has a significant, positive effect on the long-run earnings of military enlistees. We explore one hypothesis for this effect by employing similar methods to estimate the effect of enlistment on educational attainment, the idea being that the effect of enlistment on earnings could be due in part to its intermediate effect on educational attainment. Those analyses imply that enlistment increases two-year degree attainment among all enlistees, but lowers four-year degree attainment among the highest-aptitude enlistees. However, the magnitude of these education effects is too small to fully explain the long-run earnings gains attributable to enlistment.

We note here that the focus of this research is on the overall effect of enlistment on earnings and educational attainment rather than the effect of particular characteristics of military service, such as years of service and military occupation. Although the effects of these characteristics on long-run labor market outcomes are of significant interest to policymakers, the empirical strategy we employ in this research is not tailored to estimating their causal effect. Which military occupation an enlistee chooses and how long that enlistee remains in service are likely correlated with a host of unobservable characteristics of the enlistee that are themselves correlated with labor market outcomes and that are likely not controlled for by observable characteristics of the enlistee at the time of application.

The remainder of this report has the following structure. Chapter Two describes the basic empirical approach we employ to estimate the effect of enlistment on earnings and educational attainment, and discusses its limitations. Chapters Three and Four then report the estimated effect of Army enlistment on earnings and educational attainment, respectively.[8] These chapters describe specific empirical models and the data employed to estimate those models. In both chapters, we report the average estimated effect of Army enlistment over all enlistees by

---

[8] Earnings results for other services are presented in the appendix.

years since enlistment and then according to a variety of applicant characteristics, including year of application, aptitude, race/ethnicity, and gender. Chapter Five concludes by summarizing the main empirical results of this research and discussing how they might inform military manpower policy.

CHAPTER TWO
Methods and Data

We seek to estimate the causal effect of enlistment on earnings and educational attainment. This chapter details our basic empirical model, beginning with a discussion of the institutional details that motivate our approach. We reserve discussion of modeling details specific to each outcome, including a description of data on earnings and educational attainment, for Chapters Three and Four.

Enlistment, Reenlistment, and Military Compensation

In this section, we briefly discuss a number of institutional details concerning military enlistment, compensation, and separation that motivate our empirical model and are necessary for interpreting our empirical estimates.

An individual interested in joining the military begins the formal application process by visiting a military entrance processing station. Applicants who satisfy aptitude, education, health, citizenship, criminal background, and other "moral" standards are offered the opportunity to enlist. This process is managed by goals for the fraction of recruits who are high school graduates and satisfy threshold scores on the Armed Forces Qualification Test (AFQT), and by a formal system of waivers for those not satisfying current enlistment standards (see Asch, Hosek, and Martin [2009] for a more detailed discussion of enlistment standards).

Qualified applicants receive an offer, consisting of initial rank, bonus, educational benefits, military occupation and training, and initial term of service, which varies with the applicant's characteristics and military requirements at that point in time. The applicant can select one of the offered options or choose not to enlist. Those who choose one of the offered options sign a formal enlistment contract and enter the Future Soldier Training Program, also known as the Delayed Entry Program (DEP). Some enlistees begin military service within a short time of signing their contract. More typically, given personal circumstances, military needs, and the availability of specific training slots, others ship for basic training some months later. A small fraction of individuals drop from DEP and so never formally access into the military.

In this analysis, we limit our examination of military compensation to cash compensation: a combination of basic pay, cash allowances for food and housing, other smaller and less common pays and allowances, and a tax advantage due to the exclusion of all allowances and some pays from federal (and often state) income taxes. Military compensation varies with rank, years of service, and family structure (marital status, presence of children). In 2011, the average enlistee with no dependents could expect to receive about $34,000 in cash compensation in his or her first year of service.[1]

The enlistment contract specifies the period of initial service. That contract length varies with service, over time, and across individuals. As we describe below, a large fraction of enlistees separate from the military at the end of their first enlistment contract (generally three to six years in duration). At the end of the first enlistment contract, individuals choose whether to reenlist in the military or to separate and enter the civilian sector. This decision reflects both the service member's preferences and the military's decision concerning its need for the individual's continued service and the individual's suitability for continued service.

The military offers generous retirement benefits, which generate strong financial incentives to remain in the military once service members have committed to more than one or two terms of service. Another important determinant of the likelihood of reenlisting is how successful service members have been in the military. A key marker of success in the military is the speed at which one has been promoted up the military ranks. Prior evidence (Hosek and Martorell, 2009) suggests that individuals who have been promoted quickly are much more likely to reenlist in the military.

Empirical Approach

For a given individual, the causal effect of enlistment on a particular outcome (e.g., earnings, educational attainment) can be expressed as

$$R_{it} = Y_{it}^{E} - Y_{it}^{NE}, \tag{2.1}$$

where Y_{it}^{E} denotes the outcome of applicant i in the tth year since applying for military service if the applicant enlists, and Y_{it}^{NE} denotes the same outcome if the applicant never enlists. Since, for any individual applicant, it is impossible to observe the difference R_{it} (i.e., an applicant cannot both enlist and never enlist), we must estimate this difference using data on a population of individuals that enlists and a population of individuals that does not enlist.

The average effect of enlistment on a population of enlistees (generically referred to as the effect of "treatment on the treated") can be expressed as:

$$R_{t}^{E} = E(Y_{it}^{E} \mid D_{i} = 1) - E(Y_{it}^{NE} \mid D_{i} = 1), \tag{2.2}$$

where D_i is an indicator variable for enlistment. We can generate an unbiased estimate of the first term on the right-hand side of Equation 2.2 using data on enlistees. It is likely, however, that using data on individuals who never enlist will result in biased estimates of the second term on the right-hand side of Equation 2.2, the mean outcome of enlistees had they never enlisted (i.e., the counterfactual). This bias results from the fact that individuals choose to enlist in the military and the military chooses which applicants can enlist, and these choices are likely conditional on characteristics of individuals correlated with the outcomes of interest. For example, enlistment might be relatively more common among individuals with a high

[1] U.S. average for an E-1 based in the continental United States with one year of service and no dependents (see the Office of the Secretary of Defense, no date).

tolerance for risk, and the military requires enlistees to meet specific aptitude, health, drug and alcohol, and other requirements.

Comparisons of mean outcomes made conditional on the characteristics of individuals that determine enlisted status yield a causal estimate of the effect of enlistment on outcomes if the distribution of potential outcomes is unrelated to enlistment conditional on covariates included in the model. Formally, if we assume the pair $(Y_{it}^{E}, Y_{it}^{NE})$ is independent from $D_{it} \mid X_{it}$ for some vector of covariates X, then

$$R_{t}^{E} = E(Y_{it}^{E} \mid D_{i} = 1, X_{it}) - E(Y_{it}^{NE} \mid D_{i} = 0, X_{it}), \tag{2.3}$$

which we can estimate directly from data on enlistees and non-enlistees, is an unbiased estimate of the causal effect of enlistment on outcome Y. Sample size and data processing issues lead to different implementations of Equation 2.3 for our two outcomes, earnings and educational attainment. These differences are explained in Chapters Three and Four.

The key assumption in Equation 2.3 is that the vector X contains all factors that co-vary with enlistment and outcome X. We argue, as in Angrist (1998), that restricting our sample to military applicants and employing the rich data on the applicant record make this assumption plausible for our purposes. It is reasonable to assume that enlistees will be more similar to applicants who do not enlist than to individuals in the general population. This is likely to be true in terms of both observable characteristics, such as age, gender, and education, and unobservable characteristics, such as attitudes toward risk and authority. By restricting our sample to applicants, we implicitly control in X for differences in observable and unobservable characteristics across applicants and non-applicants. Within the pool of applicants, there are likely to remain important differences between applicants who do and do not enlist, but we assume that we can control for these remaining differences by employing data available in the applicant record (see later in this chapter for more discussion of this particular assumption). Thus, focusing our analysis on applicants allows us to control more completely for differences between enlistees and non-enlistees in the population at large and therefore improve our estimate of the causal effect on enlistment on earnings and education in the general population.

Data

We obtained data on military applicants from DoD Military Entrance Processing Command (MEPCOM) administrative records. These data files contain electronic records for every individual who submits a formal application for active-component military service. The extract we employ covers the universe of individuals who applied for military service between FY1989 and FY2003. We restrict our analysis file to the typical qualified applicant: individuals who were 17 and older at the time they applied for military service, had no prior military service, obtained a score of 31 or higher on the AFQT (very few individuals who score below this percentile are admitted to the military), had at most a high school diploma (excluding those with varying levels of postsecondary education), and had no potentially disqualifying health conditions or potentially disqualifying drug or alcohol use.[2] These sample restrictions leave us with

[2] Approximately 23 percent of the applicant records are missing health and drug and alcohol information. These records were dropped from the analysis.

2,763,410 applicants, or about 184,227 applicants per fiscal year, representing 45 percent of the total universe of individuals applying for military service in those years.[3]

For each applicant, the MEPCOM data include measures of the key factors the military uses to screen applicants at the time of application. In addition to the screening criteria mentioned in the previous paragraph, these measures include AFQT score (a powerful predictor of labor market earnings—see, for example, Neal and Johnson [1996])[4] and educational attainment. The application record also contains standard demographic information, such as gender, race/ethnicity, date of application, and active-component service to which the individual applied. Table 2.1 reports the mean of these applicant characteristics across all application years and all active-component services. (Table 2.2 reports the same statistics for the Army alone.)

We define an applicant as having enlisted if, according to MEPCOM records, that individual accesses following his or her application date. To "access" means that the military inducts the individual into military service. An enlistee, by this definition, could serve as little as a single day in the active component, although 92 percent of applicants in our data serve at least six months and 70 percent serve three or more years (see top line for all services in Figure 2.1). Thus, our estimates represent the average effect of serving in the active component, regardless of how long, on earnings and educational outcomes in a given year following application. It is also important to remember that a sizable fraction of active-component enlistees will continue to serve in the reserve components and so, separation from active-component service does not necessarily mean separation from military service altogether.

Limitations of Our Approach

Although our methods allow us to control for many of the factors that lead individuals to apply for military service and the military to admit those individuals, we acknowledge that differences could remain. A qualified applicant who chooses to enlist could differ from a qualified applicant who does not enlist for reasons unrelated to their propensity to apply or differences in available covariates. For example, it is plausible that, even among applicants, individuals with a higher willingness to accept the regimentation, strenuous physical work, and danger that can be associated with military employment are more likely to enlist. If these characteristics are correlated with labor market earnings, then our estimates could be biased even after adjusting for the extensive set of controls we use here.

Two other such factors are the stochastic arrival of civilian job offers (or job losses) and school admissions. Given our extensive controls, we assume that applicants who do and do not enlist are equally well prepared for civilian jobs and postsecondary education, but there is nonetheless a random component to job offers and school admissions. Take two equally well-qualified applicants. One applicant randomly receives an attractive civilian job offer and

[3] Approximately 10 percent of the sample has two or more application records indicating that their first application was suspended. This could happen either because the applicant decided to withdraw his or her application or because the applicant did not meet enlistment criteria at that time. For individuals who decide to apply again at a later date, we apply sample restrictions and measure all covariates at the time of that individual's last application record in the MEPCOM data.

[4] AFQT scores are derived from selected scores on the eight-component Armed Services Vocational Aptitude Battery (ASVAB).

Table 2.1
Mean and Standard Deviation of Applicant Characteristics: All Active-Component Applicants

Characteristic	All	Non-Enlistees	Enlistees
Enlisted	0.79	0.00	1.00
Education			
Dropout or GED	0.06	0.06	0.06
In high school	0.38	0.44	0.36
High school graduate	0.56	0.49	0.58
Male	0.82	0.77	0.84
AFQT category			
Category I	0.04	0.04	0.04
Category II	0.37	0.36	0.37
Category IIIA	0.28	0.28	0.29
Category IIIB	0.31	0.33	0.30
Race			
White	0.66	0.65	0.66
Black	0.17	0.16	0.17
Hispanic	0.09	0.09	0.09
Other	0.08	0.10	0.08
Service			
Army	0.36	0.37	0.36
Air Force	0.17	0.14	0.18
Marine Corps	0.18	0.21	0.18
Navy	0.28	0.29	0.28
Age			
17	0.27	0.29	0.26
18	0.27	0.26	0.27
19	0.17	0.14	0.17
20	0.10	0.09	0.10
21	0.06	0.06	0.07
22	0.04	0.04	0.04
23	0.03	0.03	0.03
24+	0.07	0.08	0.06
Number of observations	2,763,410	2,192,220	571,190

NOTES: Applicant characteristics also include year of application, which is not shown here. GED = General Education Development certificate.

Table 2.2
Mean and Standard Deviation of Applicant Characteristics: Army Applicants

Characteristic	All	Non-Enlistees	Enlistees
Enlisted	0.79	0.00	1.00
Education			
Dropout or GED	0.09	0.10	0.09
In high school	0.34	0.40	0.33
High school graduate	0.57	0.50	0.59
Male	0.80	0.73	0.82
AFQT category			
Category I	0.04	0.04	0.04
Category II	0.34	0.33	0.35
Category IIIA	0.29	0.28	0.30
Category IIIB	0.32	0.34	0.32
Race			
White	0.64	0.64	0.64
Black	0.20	0.19	0.20
Hispanic	0.08	0.08	0.08
Other	0.08	0.08	0.08
Age			
17	0.25	0.27	0.24
18	0.24	0.23	0.25
19	0.16	0.14	0.17
20	0.10	0.09	0.11
21	0.07	0.07	0.07
22	0.05	0.05	0.05
23	0.03	0.04	0.03
24+	0.09	0.12	0.08
Number of observations	1,005,723	210,499	795,224

NOTES: Sample restricted to Army applicants. Applicant characteristics also include year of application, which is not shown here.

the other does not. All else equal, it is reasonable to assume that the applicant receiving this job offer is less likely to enlist than the applicant who does not receive such an offer. The same might be true of school admissions. If this "good luck" has a lasting, beneficial effect on civilian labor market outcomes and postsecondary education, then Equation 2.3 will tend to underestimate the causal effect of military service on outcomes. By the same token, an individual who loses his job during the application process might be more likely to join the military.

While theoretically plausible, there are two reasons why we might expect the stochastic arrival of job offers and school admissions to be practically unimportant in this context. First, our sample has already applied for military service, and so the job offer or offer of school admission must arrive between the time the individual goes through the application process

Figure 2.1
Fraction of Enlistees Serving in the Active Component, by Years Since Application

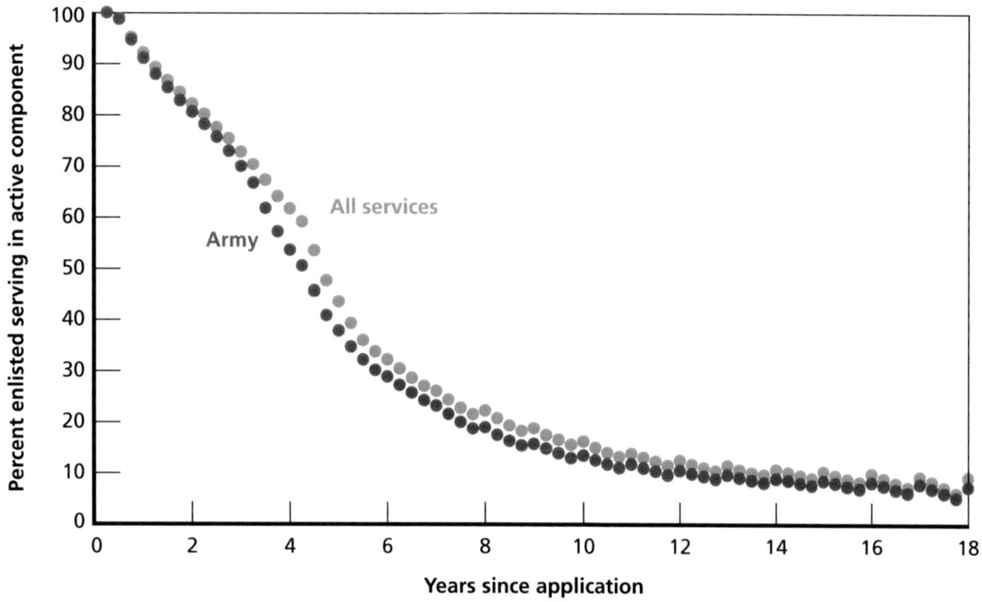

NOTES: Sample restricted to enlistees applying for active-duty service between 1989 and 2003. The percentage remaining in-service does not fall monotonically because separation rates vary slightly across cohorts.
RAND *TR995-2.1*

(which entails visiting a military entrance processing station, taking the ASVAB, completing a physical exam, and undergoing drug testing and criminal background checks) and when that individual makes the decision whether to enlist. This window is typically relatively short; the median number of months between application and enlistment in our sample is six. Second, these stochastic events must have a lasting effect on labor market outcomes and educational attainment. That is, the effect of landing a good job following high school or being admitted to a good school by chance must persist and not be countered by equally probable "bad luck" in the future.

We conclude this chapter by acknowledging two related limitations inherent in our approach. First, we estimate the effect of ever having enlisted on outcomes rather than the effect of a specific length of military service on outcomes. Although we observe years of military service in our data, it is less plausible that the covariates available on the applicant record are sufficient to control for differences between enlistees who serve for different periods of time. Put another way, over time, the pool of enlistees still serving in the active component becomes increasingly select, both because those individuals are choosing to remain in service and because the military wants them to remain in service. Thus, while it is of considerable interest to understand how characteristics of military service, such as years of service or military occupational specialty, affect outcomes, estimating such effects requires isolating exogenous variation in those characteristics, which is beyond the scope of this research.

Second, and related to the first point, we cannot isolate the effect of enlistment on the labor market outcomes of enlistees who separate from the active component. We might like to know whether civilian labor market outcomes of enlistees are affected by enlisting, but the decision to separate from the active component is endogenous, leading to potential bias for the reasons given above. We elaborate on this issue in Chapter Three.

CHAPTER THREE
The Effect of Army Enlistment on Labor Market Earnings

We begin this chapter by describing the earnings data employed in this research and explaining precisely how we estimate Equation 2.3 when the outcome in question is labor market earnings. We then report and discuss overall earnings estimates by years since application and by various applicant characteristics. In this chapter and in Chapter Four, we focus on Army enlistment. We present results for other active-component services in the appendix.

Earnings Data

Our measure of earnings includes all cash compensation received by enlistees and non-enlistees from virtually all military and civilian sources. Earnings data employed in this research come from two sources: the Social Security Administration (SSA) and the Defense Manpower Data Center (DMDC). SSA records in its Master Earnings File (MEF) earnings from all sources subject to Medicare taxes, which covers almost all U.S. employers.[1] These earnings records have been used in many empirical studies, including several studies related to the military (for example, Angrist, 1990; Angrist, 1998; and Angrist and Krueger, 1994).

Not included in SSA earnings records are military allowances (e.g., Basic Allowance for Subsistence [BAS], Basic Allowance for Housing [BAH], Family Separation Allowance [FSA]) and bonuses, which are not subject to Medicare taxes. To account for these significant sources of military earnings, we add these quantities to SSA earnings using individual-level pay records contained in DMDC's Active and Reserve Duty Pay Files. Data on military allowances and bonuses are first available starting in 1994. We then make further adjustments to account for the fact that military allowances and certain military pays (e.g., those received while serving in an officially designated combat zone) are not subject to federal income taxes. Our tax imputations assume that enlisted individuals file as single with no dependents.[2] Total earnings are converted to 2005 dollars using the Consumer Price Index for All Urban Consumers (CPI-U).

---

[1] The Code of Federal Regulations, Title 20, Part 404 (see Social Security Administration, 2011), lists employment categories that are exempt from Medicare taxes. Unlike Social Security earnings, Medicare earnings are not capped at the Social Security taxable limit.

[2] The assumption that enlistees file as single with no dependents is clearly not valid. However, the impact of this assumption on our tax imputations is likely to be small, on average. On the one hand, assuming enlistees are unmarried means that spousal earnings do not affect the enlistees' marginal tax bracket. All else equal, this assumption lowers estimated taxes. On the other hand, the assumption that enlistees have no dependents reduces the number of exemptions the enlistee can declare, which raises estimated taxes. Our imputations do not account for preferential tax treatment of military pays and allowances at the state level.

We obtain these annual earnings data for 95 percent of the applicants in our baseline applicant extract for the years 1986 to 2007.[3] Thus, for individuals in our earliest applicant cohort, 1989, we can estimate the effect of enlistment on annual earnings for up to 18 years following application. Tables 3.1 and 3.2 report average earnings of Army enlistees and non-enlistees by years since application and year of application.

Although these administrative earnings records are of very high quality, several limitations deserve mention. First, prior to 1994, earnings subject to Medicare taxes data were censored above the taxable maximum level of income. In this particular application, this censoring is unlikely to pose a serious problem because the vast majority of military applicants have earnings well below the earnings limit.[4] A second issue with Medicare earnings data is that they only have information on earnings reported to SSA. Since all military pay is reported to SSA, but not necessarily all civilian earnings (i.e., "under-the-table" earnings), any such measurement error in earnings is likely to be correlated with military service, leading to upward bias of the effects of military service.

We conclude this section by emphasizing that the focus of our analysis is on the effect of enlistment on cash compensation. An analysis of the effect of enlistment on total compensation would include the value of health, deferred, and in-kind benefits. While we know exactly what those benefits are in the military context, assigning a cash-equivalent value to them is difficult. Furthermore, while we can directly observe the cash compensation of applicants that do not enlist, we do not observe their noncash benefits and so would need to impute their value using data on the availability and generosity of noncash benefits available in the civilian economy in general. Making such imputations for all of our 15 applicant cohorts is beyond the scope of this study.

We acknowledge, however, that an analysis of the effect of enlistment on total compensation could come to different conclusions than an analysis of enlistment on cash compensation. It is argued, for example, that military health benefits are more generous than those available to the vast majority of civilian workers (Hosek et al., 2005). Under current policy, enlistees pay no premium, deductible, or co-payment; civilian health plans with such terms are virtually nonexistent. Nearly half of all enlistees live in on-base housing free of charge. Enlistees also benefit from retirement pay accruals, state and Federal Insurance Contribution Act (FICA) tax advantages, meals, commissary benefits, educational benefits, and other in-kind benefits and services. The Tenth Quadrennial Review of Military Compensation estimated the total annual value of health, retirement, and state and FICA tax advantages to be between $4,400 and $16,100 for enlisted personnel (the value grows with years of military service), which is considerably less than the imputed value of these benefits to comparably educated civilian workers (OUSD P&R, 2008). Thus, it is possible that estimates of the effect of enlistment on cash-compensation underestimate the effect of enlistment on total compensation, especially in the first few years following application, when the majority of enlistees are still serving in the active component.

---

[3] Virtually all military applicants should appear in the SSA data. All enlistees should appear in the MEF since basic pay is subject to Medicare tax, and almost all applicants will be employed in a covered job at some point in their lives. Match rates below 100 percent, therefore, are likely due to discrepancies in the names, Social Security Numbers, and dates of birth used to match the applicant and SSA records.

[4] In 1992 and 1993, the Medicare taxable earnings maximum was about $125,000 (in nominal dollars). Between 1989 and 1991, the Medicare taxable maximum was about $50,000 and was equal to the maximum for Social Security taxes. In 1990, few covered male workers had earnings that were above the Social Security taxable limit. That outcome was even less common among the young men who applied for military service.

Table 3.1
Mean Annual Earnings ($ thousands), by Years Since Application and Year of Application: Army Enlistees

Years Since Application	Application Year														
	1989	1990	1991	1992	1993	1994	1995	1996	1997	1998	1999	2000	2001	2002	2003
0						7.9	7.8	7.9	8.2	7.9	8.8	9.5	9.9	9.1	12.0
1					14.4	14.1	14.0	14.0	14.7	14.3	15.7	16.3	18.8	18.5	22.2
2				18.1	18.3	18.1	18.0	18.6	18.8	18.8	19.1	21.3	23.8	24.4	26.2
3			19.6	19.4	19.4	19.7	20.2	20.4	20.8	20.9	22.6	24.2	26.0	27.4	29.2
4		19.4	20.1	19.8	20.1	20.9	21.4	21.9	22.0	23.0	24.5	24.8	27.0	28.7	28.4
5	18.9	20.0	20.7	20.7	21.7	22.4	23.0	23.0	23.4	24.6	24.9	25.5	26.9	27.9	
6	20.3	21.1	22.3	22.8	23.7	24.5	24.4	24.5	25.4	26.0	26.9	26.6	27.6		
7	21.8	23.1	24.7	24.8	25.9	25.9	25.8	26.6	27.2	28.2	28.2	28.2			
8	23.7	25.4	26.8	27.0	27.2	27.2	27.8	28.6	29.3	29.5	29.4				
9	26.0	27.7	29.2	28.4	28.6	29.3	29.8	30.6	30.4	30.7					
10	28.2	30.1	30.5	29.6	30.4	31.3	31.8	31.7	31.8						
11	30.3	31.3	31.7	31.5	32.2	33.1	33.0	33.2							
12	31.2	32.3	33.2	33.2	33.8	34.4	34.6								
13	32.1	33.8	35.0	34.7	35.2	35.8									
14	33.4	35.5	36.5	36.1	36.6										
15	35.6	37.4	38.5	38.1											
16	36.5	38.5	39.6												
17	37.3	39.3													
18	38.3														

NOTES: Sample restricted to Army applicants who ever enlisted. Earnings ($2005) include allowances and bonuses. Total earnings data span between 1994 and 2007, which accounts for the blank cells.

Table 3.2
Mean Annual Earnings ($ thousands), by Years Since Application and Year of Application: Army Non-Enlistees

Years Since Application	Application Year 1989	1990	1991	1992	1993	1994	1995	1996	1997	1998	1999	2000	2001	2002	2003
0						7.2	7.5	7.4	7.6	7.4	8.0	8.6	8.1	7.2	8.0
1					10.3	10.7	10.7	11.1	11.3	11.1	11.6	11.7	10.5	11.7	16.1
2				12.9	13.0	13.3	13.9	14.5	14.4	14.3	14.0	13.7	13.0	15.9	21.0
3			14.9	15.0	15.0	15.9	16.7	17.0	16.8	15.7	15.2	15.2	15.3	18.9	24.7
4		16.0	17.0	17.0	17.4	18.5	19.1	19.4	18.1	16.7	16.4	16.8	17.6	21.3	25.6
5	17.2	18.1	19.1	19.5	20.2	21.0	21.4	21.0	19.3	18.1	18.1	18.4	19.6	22.6	
6	19.3	20.2	21.6	22.4	22.8	23.6	22.9	21.8	20.4	19.6	19.9	20.3	21.2		
7	21.1	22.8	24.4	24.8	25.0	24.7	23.6	23.1	22.0	21.2	21.7	22.1			
8	23.4	25.6	26.7	27.1	26.1	25.5	24.6	24.4	23.3	22.8	23.3				
9	26.1	28.1	28.7	28.1	26.6	26.4	26.1	25.8	25.1	24.4					
10	28.5	30.1	29.7	28.3	27.3	27.9	27.3	27.1	26.3						
11	30.1	30.8	30.3	29.0	28.6	29.2	28.6	28.1							
12	30.7	30.9	31.1	30.2	29.5	30.7	29.6								
13	30.8	31.4	32.0	31.2	30.9	32.1									
14	31.2	32.6	32.9	32.3	31.8										
15	32.5	33.3	33.8	33.3											
16	33.3	34.1	34.6												
17	34.3	34.9													
18	35.3														

NOTES: Sample restricted to Army applicants who ever enlisted. Earnings ($2005) include allowances and bonuses. Total earnings data span between 1994 and 2007, which accounts for the blank cells.

Earnings Model Specification

Large sample sizes allow us to estimate Equation 2.3—the effect of enlistment on annual earnings—within narrowly defined groups. In doing so, we need not maintain the relatively stringent assumption of homogeneous treatment effects across groups (where "treatment" in this context refers to enlistment). Our analysis groups, 36,458 in all, are defined by the full interaction of the covariates listed in Table 2.1 along with a variable measuring pre-application earnings (an indicator variable for having earnings above the median in a given cell).[5] In the tables and figures below, we report the estimated effect of enlistment on annual earnings at various levels of aggregation by taking weighted averages of the appropriate group-level treatment effects where the weights are given by the distribution of enlisted individuals across the groups.

As will be seen below, the estimated effect of enlistment varies considerably across enlistees with different characteristics. To isolate the effect of a particular characteristic (e.g., AFQT score), holding all other characteristics constant, in some instances we also report the weighted average treatment effect within a given group where the weights hold the distribution of other characteristics constant across the groups of interest. For example, if there were just two characteristics of interest, AFQT and age at application, we would report the weighted average treatment effect across AFQT categories assuming the same age distribution across all groups (e.g., the age distribution of all enlistees). In that way, the differences in treatment effects observed across AFQT categories reflect something about AFQT rather than something about age, which could be correlated with AFQT.

Results

We begin our presentation of earnings results by focusing on individuals who applied for military service in 1989. This applicant cohort permits the longest follow-up (18 years following application). As will be seen in the remainder of this chapter, this broad pattern of results holds across all applicant cohorts in our data. We then disaggregate estimates by year of application, AFQT category, race/ethnicity, and gender. Finally, we show how the estimated effect of Army enlistment on earnings varies by whether the enlistee is still serving in the Army. As noted in Chapter Two, the interpretation of these particular results is complicated by the fact that length of active-component service is endogenous to labor market outcomes, but the large differences we observe between these two groups deserve highlighting regardless.

1989 Applicant Cohort

Figure 3.1 graphs the estimated effect of Army enlistment on annual earnings for individuals applying for active-component service in 1989. In the figure, data points above the horizontal line at zero indicate a positive effect of enlistment on earnings, and points below that line indicate a negative effect of enlistment on earnings. The bottom line graphs the estimated effect

---

[5] There are a total of 119,912 analysis groups given the covariates listed in Table 2.1 with the addition of the pre-application earnings variable that have at least one applicant. To protect the confidentiality of individuals with Medicare-covered earnings, SSA suppresses output for groups of fewer than five individuals. In our case, this forced us to drop cells with fewer than five observations that were matched to the SSA data. SSA returned output for 62,934 cells. We then further restricted the sample to 36,458 groups for which there was "common support" for both enlistees and non-enlistees. These groups represent 2.37 million observations, or 85 percent of the original sample.

Figure 3.1
Estimated Effect of Army Enlistment on Annual Earnings ($2005), by Years Since Application: 1989 Applicant Cohort

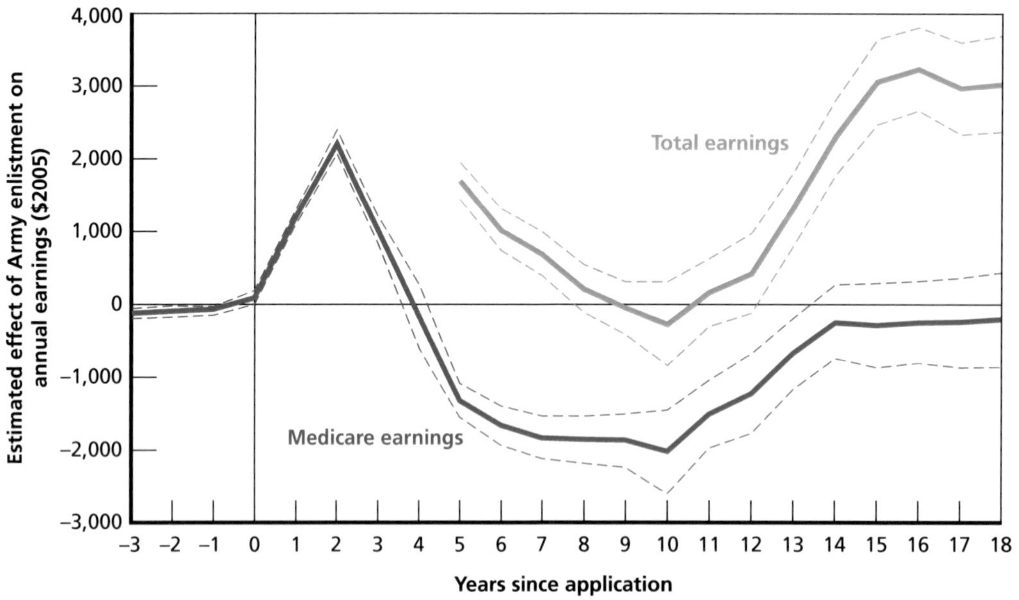

NOTES: Sample restricted to individuals applying for active-duty Army service in 1989. Dashed lines denote 95 percent confidence intervals.
RAND *TR995-3.1*

of enlistment on earnings subject to Medicare taxes (which excludes military allowances and bonuses), by years since application, where year 0 is the year of application. The top line graphs the estimated effect of Army enlistment on total earnings, including military allowances and bonuses not recorded in SSA data. As can be seen, the top line starts in year 5 for the 1989 cohort (corresponding to calendar year 1994), the first year for which we could obtain data on military bonuses and allowances. The dashed lines denote the estimated 95 percent confidence interval surrounding these estimates.

Since we control for differences in pre-application earnings, applicants who do and not enlist have nearly identical earnings prior to the year of application by design. In the first three to four years following application (years 0–3) the chart shows a strong positive effect of Army enlistment on earnings. The positive estimated effect of enlistment peaks two years following application and then declines through the ninth year following application.

The strong positive effect of enlistment on earnings in the first few years following enlistment likely reflects, in part, the need for the military to pay a compensating wage differential to attract young men and women to endure the hardships of military service. Some of the pattern in earnings effects we observe in Figure 3.1, though, also likely reflects differences in the timing of postsecondary education between enlistees and non-enlistees. In the years immediately following application, enlistees are working full-time in an occupation that pays relatively well for someone with only a high school education. Had these individuals not enlisted, some fraction of them would have attended college instead and, as a result, likely been working less than full-time and, consequently, earning comparatively little. By three years following application, however, a large fraction of enlistees will have separated from the active component. Many of these individuals will attend college when they separate and presumably work relatively little in those years. Meanwhile, had these individuals never enlisted, they would have begun their schooling several years earlier. As we will see in Chapter Four, the estimated effect of Army enlistment on college enrollment is broadly consistent with this hypothesis.

Differences in civilian employment and work experience are also likely to contribute to the pattern of estimated earnings effects. Military employment offers stable full-time work, whereas the civilian jobs individuals typically hold in the first few years after high school are characterized by high turnover. Between four and eight years following application, when enlistees are separating from the active component in large numbers, those who do not go to college enter civilian jobs with less civilian work experience than they otherwise would have, which could lead to lower earnings, all else equal.

Focusing on total earnings starting in year 5, we see that the estimated effect of enlistment continues to decline through year 10 but is nonetheless always positive (or at least statistically indistinguishable from zero). In year 11, the estimated effect of Army enlistment on total annual earnings begins to increase again and, by 18 years following application (the last year in our data) amounts to $3,016, or 8.5 percent of average non-enlistee earnings.

The earnings estimates graphed in Figure 3.1 differ from those reported in Angrist (1998) in two important ways. First, Angrist's estimates extend as many as 12 years following enlistment. At that point, the estimated effect of enlistment on earnings for the 1989 applicant cohort (and, as we will see, all applicant cohorts in our data) is becoming positive and trending upward. The analyses reported here suggest that the estimated effect of enlistment on longer-run earnings does not stabilize until 15 years following application. Second, it is clear from the figure that not accounting for allowances and bonuses, as in Angrist (1998), exerts a substantial downward bias on the estimated effect of enlistment on earnings. Consequently, from here forward and in the appendix, we report estimates for total earnings only.

Application Year

Our estimates imply that the estimated effect of Army enlistment on earnings varies considerably across applicant cohorts (see Table 3.3). There are at least two reasons why we might observe such variation over time. If military compensation is relatively slow to respond to changes in civilian economic growth, then military earnings will tend to rise relative to civilian earnings when the civilian economy is in recession, both because civilian unemployment lowers annual civilian earnings and because military wages are relatively unresponsive to decreases in civilian labor demand. When the civilian economy is growing, by contrast, military earnings will tend to fall relative to civilian earnings. In the longer run, however, military pay must adjust to account for growth in the civilian economy in order to attract and retain the required force. For example, facing a difficult recruiting and retention environment due to a strong civilian economy, Congress in 2000 authorized substantial increases in basic pay and the basic allowance for housing that pushed military cash compensation to the 70th percentile of the civilian earnings distribution for comparably aged and educated individuals (Asch, Hosek, and Martin, 2002; OUSD P&R, 2008). We do not report tests of these hypotheses here, but the pattern of estimates evident in Table 3.3 is broadly consistent with the hypothesis that short-run earnings effects are larger in periods of high civilian unemployment and that these short-run earnings effects are largest for the 1998–2003 cohorts, which benefited from the increase in basic pay in 2000.

Figure 3.2 graphs the estimated effect of enlistment on earnings across all 15 applicant cohorts and its associated 95 percent confidence interval by years since application (Figure 3.3

Table 3.3
Estimated Effect of Army Enlistment on Annual Earnings ($2005, thousands), by Years Since Application and Year of Application

Years Since Application	Application Year 1989	1990	1991	1992	1993	1994	1995	1996	1997	1998	1999	2000	2001	2002	2003	Avg.
0						0.7	0.3	0.5	0.6	0.6	0.9	0.9	1.8	1.9	4.0	0.6
1					4.2	3.4	3.3	2.9	3.4	3.2	4.1	4.6	8.4	6.8	6.1	3.0
2				5.2	5.3	4.8	4.1	4.1	4.4	4.4	5.2	7.6	10.8	8.5	5.2	4.3
3			4.7	4.3	4.4	3.8	3.5	3.4	4.1	5.1	7.4	9.1	10.7	8.5	4.5	4.6
4		3.4	3.1	2.7	2.7	2.4	2.3	2.5	4.0	6.3	8.1	8.0	9.4	7.4	2.9	4.2
5	1.7	1.9	1.6	1.2	1.5	1.4	1.7	2.0	4.1	6.5	6.8	7.1	7.3	5.3		3.5
6	1.0	0.9	0.7	0.5	0.9	0.9	1.5	2.7	5.0	6.3	7.0	6.3	6.4			2.9
7	0.7	0.3	0.2	0.0	0.9	1.2	2.2	3.5	5.2	7.1	6.5	6.0				2.6
8	0.2	−0.2	0.1	−0.1	1.1	1.7	3.2	4.2	6.0	6.7	6.1					2.4
9	−0.1	−0.4	0.5	0.2	1.9	2.9	3.7	4.8	5.3	6.2						2.3
10	−0.3	0.0	0.8	1.3	3.1	3.5	4.5	4.5	5.5							2.3
11	0.1	0.5	1.4	2.5	3.6	3.8	4.5	5.1								2.4
12	0.4	1.4	2.1	3.0	4.3	3.7	5.0									2.6
13	1.3	2.4	2.9	3.5	4.4	3.8										2.8
14	2.2	2.8	3.6	3.8	4.8											3.3
15	3.0	4.2	4.7	4.8												4.0
16	3.2	4.5	5.0													4.1
17	3.0	4.4														3.6
18	3.0															3.0

NOTES: Sample restricted to Army applicants. Earnings include allowances and bonuses. Average treatment effect is weighted by number of enlistees in each application year.

Figure 3.2
Estimated Effect of Army Enlistment on Annual Earnings ($2005), by Years Since Application: All Applicant Cohorts

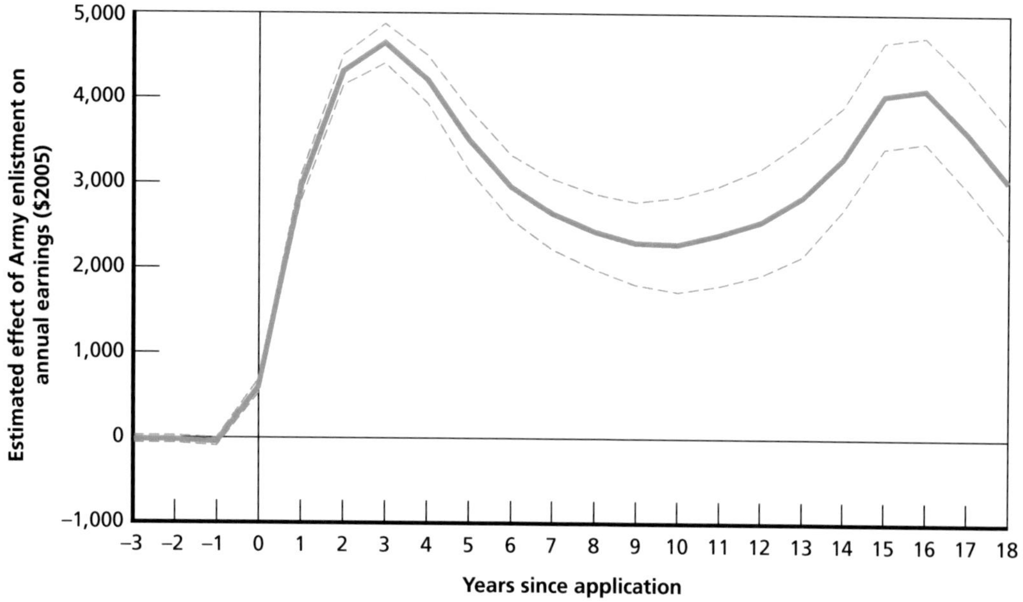

NOTES: Sample restricted to Army applicants. Dashed lines denote 95 percent confidence intervals.
RAND *TR995-3.2*

Figure 3.3
Estimated Percentage Effect of Army Enlistment on Annual Earnings, by Years Since Application: All Applicant Cohorts

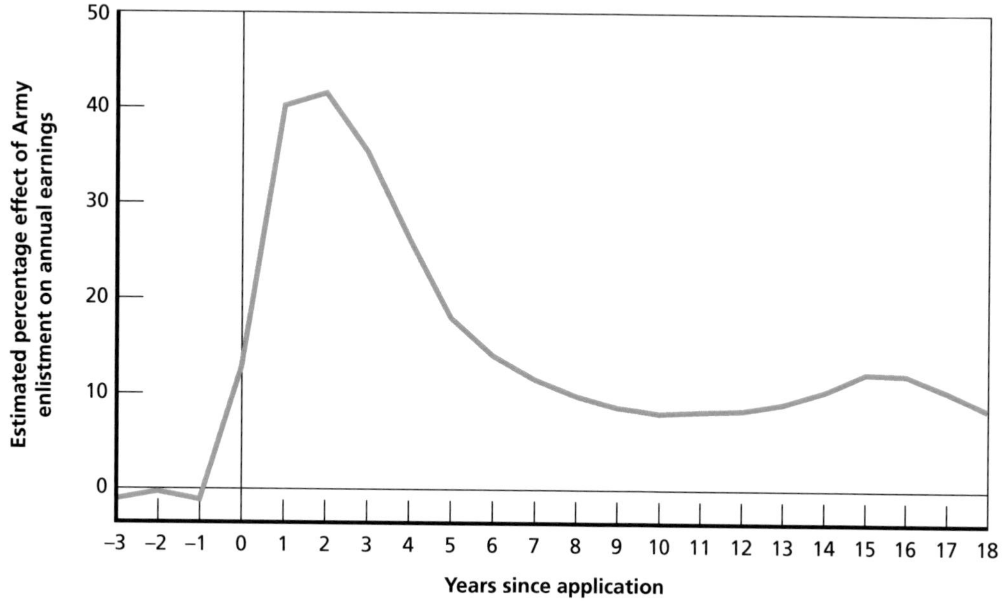

NOTES: Sample restricted to Army applicants. Percentages are computed relative to the earnings of non-enlistees.
RAND *TR995-3.3*

graphs the estimated effect as a percentage of non-enlistee earnings).[6] The positive estimated effect of enlistment peaks two years following application at 42 percent and then declines through the tenth year following application. Between 14 and 18 years following enlistment, the average effect of enlistment on annual earnings amounts to about 11 percent of average non-enlistee earnings.

Armed Forces Qualification Test

Figure 3.4 suggests that Army enlistment exerts a much stronger positive effect on the earnings of lower-aptitude enlistees than it does on the earnings of higher-aptitude enlistees. This figure shows the estimated effect of Army enlistment on annual earnings by AFQT category (Categories I and II, Category IIIA, and Category IIIB) and years since application, averaged across all applicant cohorts. Six years following application, the estimates imply that Category I and II enlistees earn somewhat more than they would have had they not enlisted. This positive effect of enlistment is positive thereafter but statistically indistinguishable from zero.

By contrast, the estimated effect of Army enlistment on Category IIIA and IIIB applicants is always positive and statistically significant. Between 14 and 18 years following application, the estimates imply that Category IIIA and IIIB enlistees earn 15 percent and 22 percent more than they would have had they never enlisted, respectively (see Table 3.4). Table 3.5 demonstrates that this pattern of results with respect to AFQT is maintained holding the distribution of other applicant characteristics constant across AFQT categories.

Figure 3.4
Estimated Percentage Effect of Army Enlistment on Annual Earnings, by Years Since Application and AFQT Category: All Applicant Cohorts

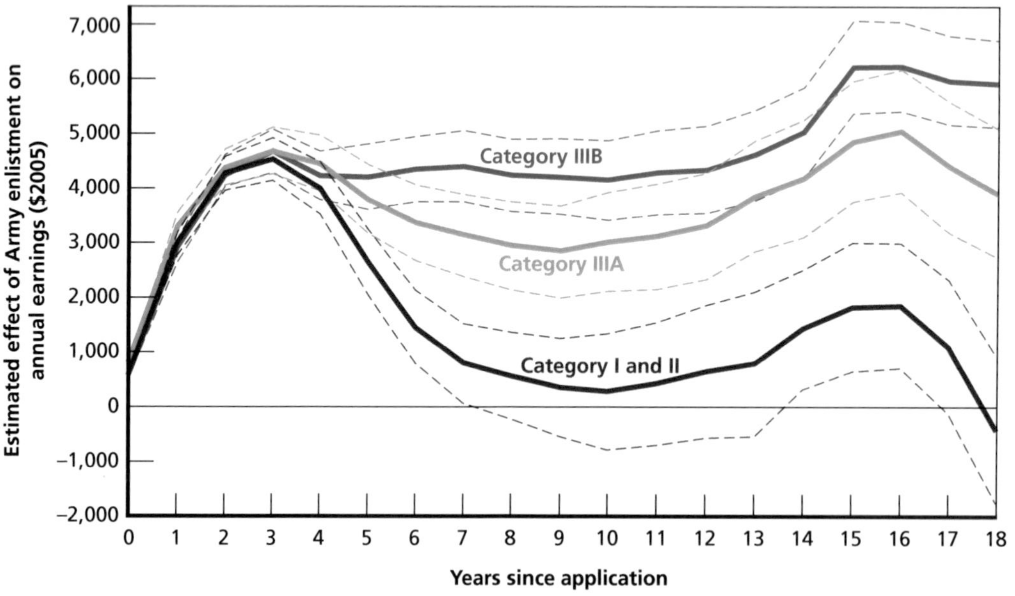

NOTES: Sample restricted to Army applicants. Dashed lines denote 95 percent confidence intervals.
RAND *TR995-3.4*

[6] Note that Figure 3.2 and the figures averaged across applicant cohorts presented below do not hold applicant cohort constant. In general, the number of applicant cohorts underlying these estimates diminishes with years since application.

Table 3.4
Estimated Effect of Army Enlistment on Earnings ($2005, thousands), by Years Since Application and AFQT Category: All Applicant Cohorts

Years Since Application	Categories I and II		Category IIIA		Category IIIB	
	Mean	Percentage	Mean	Percentage	Mean	Percentage
0	0.5	11	0.8	17	0.6	13
1	3.0	38	3.3	45	2.9	39
2	4.3	39	4.4	43	4.3	43
3	4.6	33	4.7	36	4.7	38
4	4.0	23	4.4	28	4.2	29
5	2.6	12	3.8	20	4.2	24
6	1.5	6	3.4	17	4.4	23
7	0.8	3	3.1	14	4.4	22
8	0.6	2	3.0	13	4.2	20
9	0.4	1	2.8	11	4.2	18
10	0.3	1	3.0	12	4.2	17
11	0.4	1	3.1	11	4.3	17
12	0.7	2	3.3	12	4.3	17
13	0.8	2	3.9	13	4.6	18
14	1.4	4	4.2	14	5.0	19
15	1.8	5	4.9	16	6.2	23
16	1.9	5	5.1	16	6.2	23
17	1.1	3	4.4	14	6.0	22
18	–0.5	–1	3.9	12	5.9	21

NOTES: Sample restricted to Army applicants. Earnings ($2005) include allowances and bonuses. Earnings effect is a weighted average of earnings effects over all applicant cohorts. Percentage earnings effect is relative to average non-enlistee earnings.

Race/Ethnicity and Gender

Figure 3.5 and Table 3.6 show that African American and Hispanic enlistees, on average, experience larger earnings gains from enlistment than do whites. For example, 10 years following enlistment, the estimated effect of enlistment on earnings is 22 percent for African Americans, 11 percent for Hispanics, and 5 percent for whites. African Americans and Hispanics, on average, score lower on the AFQT than do whites, and so some of these differences in earnings effects could be attributable to differences in AFQT. The results reported in Table 3.7, however, indicate that differences in earnings effects, regardless of years since activation, persist even after controlling for differences in the distribution age, gender, and AFQT scores across race/ethnicity categories. Put another way, the estimates imply that an African American or Hispanic enlistee with a given AFQT score will benefit substantially more from military service in terms of earnings than will a white enlistee with the same AFQT score.

Figure 3.6 and Tables 3.8 and 3.9 show that the overall effect of enlistment on earnings does not vary meaningfully by gender. The point estimates reported in Table 3.9 (which controls for differences in observable characteristics across the two groups) are similar in both

Table 3.5
Re-Weighted Estimated Effect of Army Enlistment on Annual Earnings ($2005, thousands), by Years Since Application and AFQT Category: All Applicant Cohorts

Years Since Application	Categories I and II		Category IIIA		Category IIIB	
	Mean	Percentage	Mean	Percentage	Mean	Percentage
0	0.7	15	0.9	21	0.7	15
1	3.3	42	3.5	48	2.9	41
2	4.8	44	4.8	47	4.4	44
3	5.1	36	5.2	40	4.7	38
4	4.7	27	4.9	31	4.2	28
5	3.5	16	4.2	22	4.0	23
6	2.2	9	3.7	19	4.1	22
7	1.3	5	3.3	15	4.1	20
8	1.1	4	3.1	13	3.8	18
9	1.0	3	2.9	11	3.7	16
10	1.0	3	2.9	11	3.7	16
11	0.8	2	3.1	11	3.9	16
12	1.2	3	3.1	11	3.8	15
13	1.9	5	3.6	13	4.2	16
14	2.7	7	4.0	13	4.5	17
15	2.9	7	4.7	16	5.8	22
16	3.4	8	5.4	17	5.9	22
17	3.0	7	5.0	16	5.6	20
18	0.6	1	5.2	16	5.9	21

NOTES: Sample restricted to Army applicants. Earnings ($2005) include allowances and bonuses. Earnings effect is a weighted average of earnings effects over all applicant cohorts employing the distribution of age, gender, and race/ethnicity of the overall Army enlisted population. Percentage earnings effect is relative to average non-enlistee earnings.

magnitude and percentage terms across gender. Moreover, these differences in point estimates are not statistically significant given the relatively large standard errors surrounding the female earnings effects (due to relatively small sample sizes).

In-Service

The results shown in Figures 3.2 and 3.3 suggest that Army enlistment has a positive effect on earnings as many as 18 years following application. As we will see in Chapter Four, although we find that Army enlistment has a positive effect on educational attainment, the estimated effects are too small to explain the large positive earnings effects we observe, especially for Category III enlistees. This leaves at least two alternative explanations. It could be that the technical expertise and soft skills developed while serving in the military exert a positive effect on long-run earnings. It could also be that military service pays particularly well and that much of the earnings gains we observe are attributable to this relatively high pay.

Figure 3.5
Estimated Percentage Effect of Army Enlistment on Annual Earnings, by Years Since Application and Race/Ethnicity

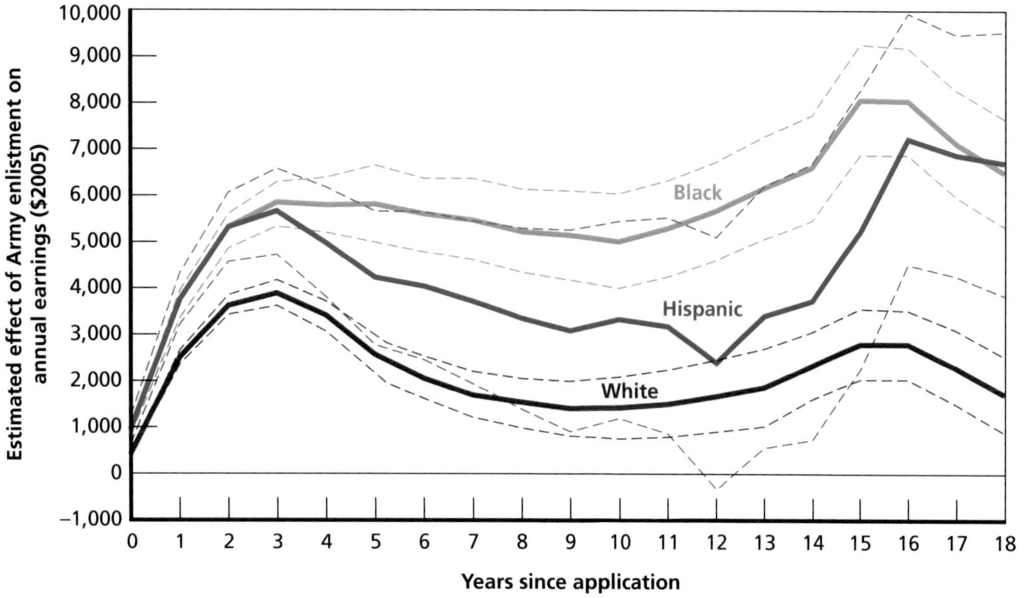

NOTES: Sample restricted to Army applicants. Dashed lines denote 95 percent confidence intervals.
RAND *TR995-3.5*

We cannot test these hypotheses directly with the data available to us in this research. However, we can decompose the estimated effect of Army enlistment on earnings into that attributable to individuals who have separated from the active component and those who remain in active-component service. Figure 3.7 graphs the result of this decomposition by AFQT category across all applicant cohorts. The figure implies that much of the positive effect of enlistment is concentrated among enlistees who continue to serve in the military. This finding is perhaps unsurprising in the early years following application, when applicants who did not enlist are much less likely to be working full-time than applicants who did enlist. But the figure suggests the positive effect of enlistment is concentrated among those enlistees who continue to serve in the military in the later years of our data as well. Eighteen years following enlistment, enlistees who continue to serve in the active component earn 78 (Category I and II), 123 (Category IIIA), and 157 (Category IIIB) percent more than applicants who never enlisted. By contrast, these earnings effects are –9 (Category I and II), 2 (Category IIIA), and 7 (Category IIIB) percent for enlistees who have separated from the active component by that year.

The earnings estimates graphed in Figure 3.7 (and summarized in Tables 3.10 and 3.11), however, cannot be interpreted causally, since enlistees who separate from the active component are likely different from enlistees who remain in-service in ways for which we cannot necessarily control given our data. Indeed, differences between enlistees who do and do not remain in-service are likely to become more extreme with years since application since, in each year, both enlistees and the military decide whether a given individual will remain in-service. On the one hand, individuals who separate may do so because they have identified promising civilian careers. On the other hand, promotion criteria become increasingly stringent as indi-

Table 3.6
Estimated Effect of Army Enlistment on Annual Earnings ($2005, thousands), by Years Since Application and Race/Ethnicity: All Applicant Cohorts

Years Since Application	White		Black		Hispanic	
	Mean	Percentage	Mean	Percentage	Mean	Percentage
0	0.5	11	0.8	21	0.9	18
1	2.5	33	3.7	58	3.8	45
2	3.7	34	5.3	61	5.3	46
3	3.9	29	5.8	54	5.7	39
4	3.4	21	5.8	44	5.0	29
5	2.5	13	5.8	36	4.2	21
6	2.1	9	5.6	31	4.1	18
7	1.7	7	5.5	29	3.7	15
8	1.5	6	5.2	25	3.3	13
9	1.4	5	5.1	23	3.1	11
10	1.4	5	5.0	22	3.3	11
11	1.5	5	5.3	22	3.2	10
12	1.7	5	5.7	23	2.4	7
13	1.9	6	6.2	25	3.4	10
14	2.4	7	6.6	26	3.7	11
15	2.8	8	8.1	31	5.3	15
16	2.8	8	8.1	30	7.2	20
17	2.3	6	7.1	26	6.9	19
18	1.7	5	6.5	23	6.7	18

NOTES: Sample restricted to Army applicants. Earnings ($2005) include allowances and bonuses. Earnings effect is a weighted average of earnings effects over all applicant cohorts. Percentage earnings effect is relative to average non-enlistee earnings.

viduals progress to higher ranks, suggesting that only the best enlistees remain serving in the active component in later years.[7] Thus, the direction of the selection bias affecting the estimates reported in Figure 3.7 and Tables 3.10 and 3.11 is unclear a priori.

It is important to note, however, that 14–18 years following application, less than 10 percent of Army enlistees are still currently serving in the active component (see lower line in Figure 2.1). Thus, the estimated effect of enlistment on the earnings of enlistees who are no longer serving in the active component in those years is likely to be relatively unaffected by selection bias. Put another way, it is unlikely that the movement of individuals from the in-service to the separated group will have a substantial impact on the average estimated effect of enlistment on the separated group simply because the number of individuals making the transition from military to civilian life in those later years is small. Thus, it may be reasonable to conclude that the longer-run earnings gains we observe for Category III enlistees who have

[7] Hosek and Mattock (2003) find that much of the variation in promotion speed is largely driven by unobservable factors and not AFQT, although Asch and Warner (2001) do find that promotion speed in the enlisted ranks is positively related to AFQT.

Table 3.7
Re-Weighted Estimated Effect of Army Enlistment on Annual Earnings ($2005, thousands), by Years Since Application and Race/Ethnicity: All Applicant Cohorts

Years Since Application	White		Black		Hispanic	
	Mean	Percentage	Mean	Percentage	Mean	Percentage
0	0.5	11	0.8	22	0.9	18
1	2.5	33	3.7	59	3.9	46
2	3.7	35	5.3	61	5.8	50
3	3.9	29	5.8	54	6.1	42
4	3.4	20	5.7	43	5.7	33
5	2.5	13	5.5	34	4.6	23
6	2.1	9	4.9	28	3.9	17
7	1.7	7	4.7	24	3.0	12
8	1.5	6	4.4	21	2.7	10
9	1.5	5	4.2	19	2.4	8
10	1.5	5	4.0	17	2.6	9
11	1.6	5	4.3	18	2.2	7
12	1.8	6	4.8	20	1.6	5
13	2.0	6	5.3	21	2.6	8
14	2.4	7	5.8	23	3.3	9
15	3.0	9	7.0	26	3.6	10
16	3.0	9	7.0	26	5.3	15
17	2.7	7	6.1	22	5.3	15
18	2.1	6	5.2	18	4.9	13

NOTES: Sample restricted to Army applicants. Earnings ($2005) include allowances and bonuses. Earnings effect is a weighted average of earnings effects over all applicant cohorts employing the distribution of age, gender, and AFQT of the overall Army enlisted population.

separated are the result of military service as opposed to factors correlated with military separation. Whether this longer-run earnings effect is attributable to gains in educational attainment, as we will see in Chapter Four, or other benefits of military service is not known.

The very large earnings effects we observe for enlistees of all aptitudes, on the other hand, are not easily interpreted. They could reflect (1) a causal effect of military service on earnings, (2) positive selection on unobservable characteristics, or (3) a compensating wage differential paid to military service members. In all likelihood all three factors contribute to the estimated in-service effects.

Figure 3.6
Estimated Percentage Effect of Army Enlistment on Annual Earnings, by Years Since Application and Gender: All Applicant Cohorts

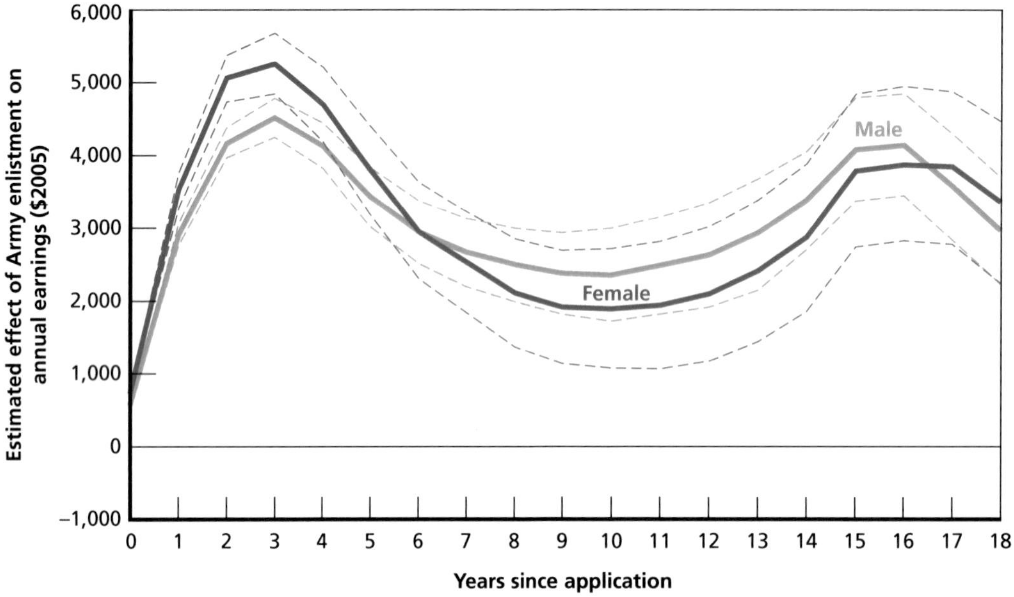

NOTES: Sample restricted to Army applicants. Dashed lines denote 95 percent confidence intervals.
RAND *TR995-3.6*

Table 3.8
Estimated Effect of Army Enlistment on Annual Earnings ($2005, thousands), by Years Since Application and Gender: All Applicant Cohorts

Years Since Application	Male		Female	
	Mean	Percentage	Mean	Percentage
0	0.6	13	0.8	18
1	2.9	38	3.5	53
2	4.2	39	5.1	57
3	4.5	33	5.3	49
4	4.1	25	4.7	37
5	3.4	17	3.8	25
6	2.9	13	3.0	18
7	2.7	11	2.5	14
8	2.5	10	2.1	11
9	2.4	9	1.9	10
10	2.4	8	1.9	9
11	2.5	8	1.9	9
12	2.6	8	2.1	9
13	2.9	9	2.4	10
14	3.4	10	2.9	12
15	4.1	12	3.8	16
16	4.1	12	3.9	16
17	3.6	10	3.8	15
18	3.0	8	3.4	13

NOTES: Sample restricted to Army applicants. Earnings ($2005) include allowances and bonuses. Earnings effect is a weighted average of earnings effects over all applicant cohorts. Percentage earnings effect is relative to average non-enlistee earnings.

Table 3.9
Re-Weighted Estimated Effect of Army Enlistment on Annual Earnings ($2005, thousands), by Years Since Application and Gender: All Applicant Cohorts

Years Since Application	Male		Female	
	Mean	Percentage	Mean	Percentage
0	0.8	16	0.9	20
1	3.2	41	3.6	54
2	4.4	42	5.3	60
3	4.8	35	5.5	51
4	4.5	27	4.9	38
5	3.9	19	3.9	26
6	3.5	16	3.1	19
7	3.2	13	2.4	14
8	3.0	11	2.1	11
9	2.8	10	1.9	9
10	2.9	10	1.9	9
11	3.0	10	1.9	9
12	3.1	10	2.0	9
13	3.6	11	2.3	10
14	4.1	12	2.9	12
15	5.1	15	3.2	13
16	5.6	16	3.2	13
17	4.9	14	3.3	13
18	4.3	12	2.8	11

NOTES: Sample restricted to Army applicants. Earnings ($2005) include allowances and bonuses. Earnings effect is a weighted average of earnings effects over all applicant cohorts employing the distribution of age, race/ethnicity, and AFQT of the overall Army enlisted population.

Figure 3.7
Estimated Effect of Army Enlistment on Annual Earnings, by Years Since Application, AFQT Category, and Whether Currently Serving in the Active Component: All Applicant Cohorts

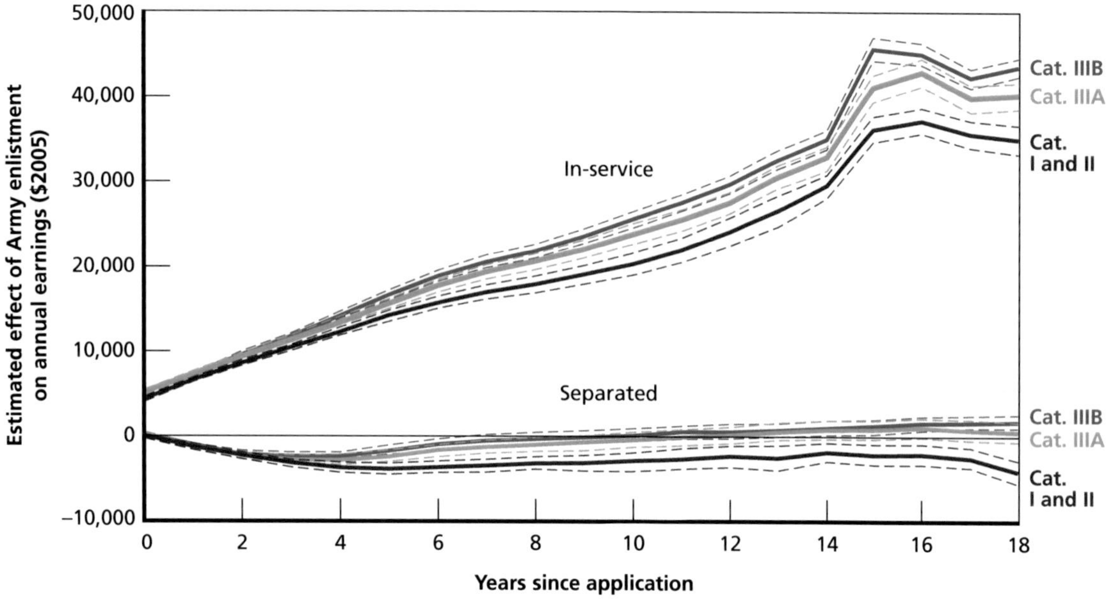

NOTES: Sample restricted to Army applicants. In-service estimates restricted to enlistees currently serving in the active component in a given year since application. Separated is restricted to enlistees who separated from the active component at any time prior to or in a given year since application. Dashed lines denote 95 percent confidence intervals.

RAND *TR995-3.7*

Table 3.10
Estimated Effect of Army Enlistment on Annual Earnings ($2005, thousands), by Years Since Application and AFQT Category Across All Applicant Cohorts: Currently Serving in the Active Component

Years Since Application	Categories I and II		Category IIIA		Category IIIB	
	Mean	Percentage	Mean	Percentage	Mean	Percentage
0	4.2	50	5.1	69	4.0	57
1	6.6	54	7.4	68	6.5	62
2	8.6	57	9.3	67	9.4	71
3	10.2	59	11.2	71	11.5	76
4	11.9	62	13.3	77	14.0	84
5	13.8	65	15.5	83	16.6	94
6	15.0	65	17.4	87	18.9	101
7	15.8	62	18.9	88	20.6	103
8	16.5	60	19.8	86	21.7	102
9	17.6	59	21.1	86	23.2	103
10	18.7	58	22.6	88	24.7	104
11	20.3	60	23.9	88	26.2	107
12	22.6	64	26.0	92	28.1	111
13	25.8	69	29.5	102	31.3	121
14	29.1	76	32.3	109	34.2	131
15	35.8	90	40.7	133	45.0	168
16	37.0	91	42.6	137	44.9	165
17	35.4	84	39.7	124	42.3	155
18	34.9	78	40.2	123	43.5	157

NOTES: Sample restricted to Army enlistees currently serving as of given year since application and all applicants who never served. Earnings ($2005) include allowances and bonuses. Earnings effect is a weighted average of earnings effects over all applicant cohorts. Percentage earnings effect is relative to average non-enlistee earnings.

Table 3.11
Estimated Effect of Army Enlistment on Annual Earnings ($2005, thousands), by Years Since Application and AFQT Category Average Across All Applicant Cohorts: Currently Separated from the Active Component

Years Since Application	Categories I and II		Category IIIA		Category IIIB	
	Mean	Percentage	Mean	Percentage	Mean	Percentage
0	0	0	0.2	3	0.1	2
1	–1.0	–8	–1.0	–9	–0.9	–8
2	–2.0	–13	–2.0	–14	–1.8	–13
3	–2.8	–16	–2.4	–15	–2.1	–13
4	–3.5	–18	–2.5	–14	–2.2	–13
5	–3.8	–18	–2.2	–12	–1.6	–9
6	–3.7	–16	–1.6	–8	–0.9	–5
7	–3.5	–14	–1.2	–6	–0.4	–2
8	–3.2	–11	–0.9	–4	–0.2	–1
9	–3.1	–10	–0.7	–3	0.0	0
10	–3.0	–9	–0.3	–1	0.2	1
11	–2.7	–8	0.0	0	0.6	2
12	–2.5	–7	0.2	1	0.7	3
13	–2.5	–7	0.6	2	0.8	3
14	–1.9	–5	0.9	3	1.2	5
15	–2.1	–5	0.9	3	1.3	5
16	–2.1	–5	1.1	3	1.7	6
17	–2.6	–6	0.8	2	1.9	7
18	–4.1	–9	0.5	2	1.9	7

NOTES: Sample restricted to Army enlistees who separted prior to or in the given year since application and all applicants who never served. Earnings ($2005) include allowances and bonuses. Earnings effect is a weighted average of earnings effects over all applicant cohorts. Percentage earnings effect is relative to average non-enlistee earnings.

CHAPTER FOUR

The Effect of Army Enlistment on Educational Attainment

In this chapter, we turn from the analysis of the effect of enlistment on earnings to the effect of enlistment on educational attainment. This chapter begins with a discussion of the National Student Clearinghouse data, which we use to identify college enrollment and degree attainment among military applicants. We then explain precisely how we estimate Equation 2.3 when the outcome in question is college enrollment and degree attainment. Finally, we report and discuss estimates of the impact of Army enlistment on current and cumulative college enrollment and degree attainment overall and by AFQT category and race/ethnicity, for both two- and four-year colleges.

Education Data

Our education data come from the National Student Clearinghouse (NSC). Founded in 1993, NSC is a nonprofit organization that contracts with institutions of higher education to verify college enrollment and degree receipt for student loan agencies. The NSC data allow us to track military applicants as they transition in and out of college and complete college degrees.

NSC maintains college enrollment data for institutions in years in which those institutions had an active contract with NSC. Between 1993 and 2010, NSC's coverage of college enrollment grew from 13 to 93 percent of all college enrollments (see Figure 4.1). NSC also maintains a degree verification service for participating institutions. In 2010, about 70 percent of all U.S. colleges participated in this service. Participating institutions submit electronic degree records for all available years. Consequently, in earlier years, coverage of college degrees is more complete than coverage of college enrollment. NSC is able to verify about 63 percent of all degrees awarded by U.S. colleges in 1991, the earliest applicant cohort employed in these analyses.

Incomplete enrollment and degree coverage in the NSC data has implications for our analysis and sample selection. First, in choosing applicant cohorts for analysis, we face a trade-off between data coverage and the ability to observe completed college enrollment and degree attainment. Selecting earlier applicant cohorts increases the likelihood that we will observe completed college enrollment and degree attainment. However, the NSC data omit a larger fraction of enrollments and degrees attained in the earlier years of this sample. Selecting later applicant cohorts provides better coverage but allows us fewer years to observe completed enrollment and degree attainment. This trade-off is more pronounced for college enrollment outcomes, the coverage of which increased sharply between 1993 and 2010.

Figure 4.1
Percentage of U.S. College Enrollment and Degrees Awarded Covered by NSC Data, by Year

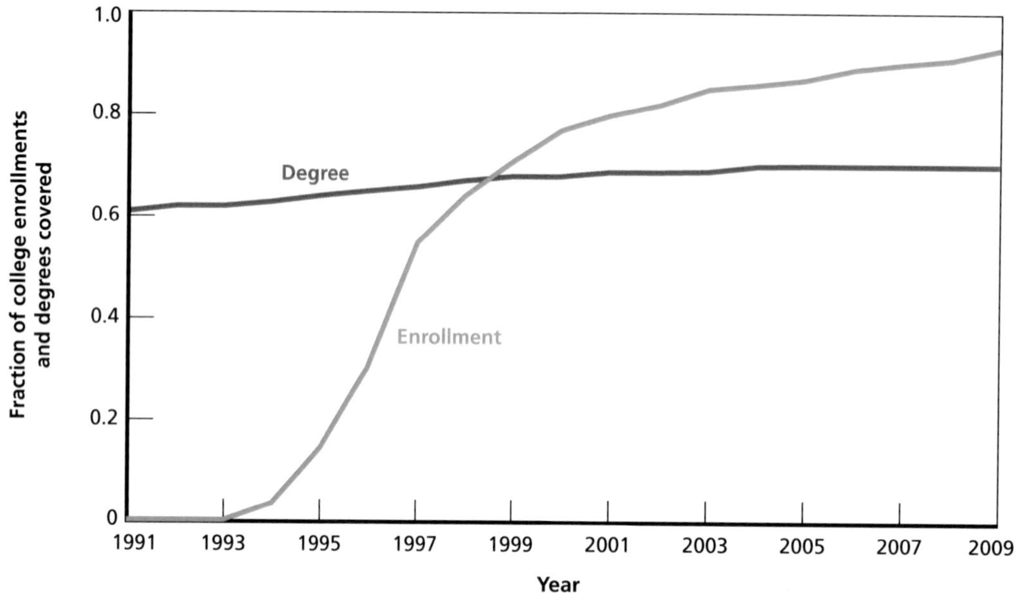

SOURCE: National Student Clearinghouse.
RAND *TR995-4.1*

Second, since we expect enlistees to delay college enrollment relative to non-enlistees, we must restrict the NSC data to colleges that are in every year of our sample so that, a priori, enlistees and non-enlistees have equal opportunity to appear as enrolled in these data. If we were to define college enrollment in a given year as being enrolled in any institution in the NSC data, we would tend to undercount college enrollment of non-enlistees relative to enlistees. This is because enlistees are likely to enroll at a later date when NSC enrollment coverage is more complete.

Based on the above considerations and the cost of obtaining data from NSC, we restrict our sample as follows. When examining college enrollment, we restrict our sample to the 1998–2000 applicant cohorts. When examining college degree attainment, we restrict our sample to the 1991–1994 applicant cohorts. Enrollment is defined as enrolling in a college that began contracting with NSC prior to 1998. College degree attainment is defined as attaining a degree from a college contracting with NSC at the time we obtained NSC's data (March 2010) and that submitted degree attainment data covering the period 1991–2010.

Employing these sample restrictions we measure 67 percent of all college enrollments for the 1998–2000 applicant cohorts and 63 percent of all awarded college degrees for the 1991–1994 applicant cohorts. These statistics imply that we underestimate college enrollment and degree attainment by approximately one-third. This underestimation poses a problem for our estimates of the effect of enlistment on education only insofar as applicants who do and do not enlist are more or less likely to attend and receive degrees from the colleges that are not in our sample. One possible concern is the fact that the NSC data only cover 20 percent of enrollments at for-profit colleges for our cohorts. The evidence suggests that veterans have a high propensity to enroll at for-profit institutions, which would cause us to underestimate the impact of enlistment on college enrollment and completion overall.

However, there is little reason to believe there would be differential enrollment at particular institutions within a given type (e.g., two-year versus four-year institutions), especially once we condition on applicant characteristics. Thus, while the means of our educational outcomes are likely to be biased downward, we assume that the difference in these outcomes between enlistees and non-enlistees, conditional on applicant covariates, is an unbiased estimate of the causal effect of enlistment on education within a given college type. The estimates reported below are for two- or four-year not-for-profit institutions only.

For this project, we obtained NSC data on enrollments and degree attainment for 120,000 male applicants in the 1991–1994 cohorts and 120,000 male applicants in the 1998–2000 cohorts (cost considerations prohibited us from obtaining data for the entire population of applicants). In order to ensure a large enough sample to detect reasonable effect sizes for well-defined subgroups, we stratified our sample by race and AFQT category, over-sampling high-aptitude Hispanics and African Americans while under-sampling low-aptitude white applicants. We also selected our sample so that half of it consists of Army applicants and the other half consists of applicants to the other three active component services. For reasons of cost, we did not purchase NSC data for female applicants. After applying the sample restrictions described in Chapter Two, we are left with 139,169 observations. Table 4.1 reports sample sizes and sampling weights used in the analyses described below.

Table 4.1
Sample Sizes and Sampling Weights for Educational Analyses

	Enrollment Cohort: 1998–2000			Degree Cohort: 1991–1994		
	Cats. I and II	Cat. IIIA	Cat. IIIB	Cats. I and II	Cat. IIIA	Cat. IIIB
A. Number of Observations						
Army						
White	4,971	5,003	4,689	5,753	5,807	5,543
Black	2,589	2,537	2,373	3,014	3,029	2,934
Hispanic	2,530	2,940	2,438	3,069	3,385	2,886
Non-Army						
White	5,640	5,748	5,544	6,446	6,592	6,388
Black	2,828	2,804	2,634	3,355	3,290	3,218
Hispanic	3,107	3,024	2,860	3,471	3,457	3,273
B. Sampling Weights						
Army						
White	8.97	5.30	4.74	5.76	3.99	4.05
Black	1.59	2.31	4.12	1.30	1.96	4.16
Hispanic	1.00	1.00	1.44	1.00	1.11	2.04
Non-Army						
White	16.96	9.36	8.91	9.54	5.90	6.07
Black	2.63	3.36	6.28	1.92	2.57	5.52
Hispanic	2.41	2.23	2.99	1.83	2.01	3.28

Education Model Specification

We estimate the effect of enlistment on educational outcomes employing the following probit model:

$$prob(Y_{it}=1)=prob(\alpha_t+\beta_t D_i+X_i\theta_t+\varepsilon_{it}>0), \qquad (4.1)$$

where Y_{it} is an indicator for whether applicant i was enrolled (or had ever enrolled) in a two- or four-year college or obtained a two- or four-year college degree in the tth year following application (see Tables 4.2 and 4.3 for means of these outcome variables for Army applicants), D_i is an indicator for whether the applicant enlisted, X_i is a vector of applicant characteristics described in Chapter Two (see Tables 2.1 and 2.2), and ε_{it} is an idiosyncratic, normally distributed error term. Y_{it} is defined for any two- or four-year college enrollment or degree, two-year college enrollment or degree, and four-year college enrollment or degree. As in Chapter Three, we investigate how the estimated effect of enlistment on educational attainment varies by AFQT category by fully interacting our AFQT control variables with enlistment and the variables in the vector X_i.

Table 4.2
Mean Educational Outcomes, by Years Since Application: Army Enlistees

Years Since Application	Current Enrollment			Cumulative Enrollment			Degree Attainment		
	All	2-Year	4-Year	All	2-Year	4-Year	All	2-Year	4-Year
0	0.09	0.07	0.03	0.09	0.07	0.03			
1	0.05	0.04	0.02	0.12	0.10	0.05			
2	0.07	0.06	0.03	0.16	0.14	0.06	0.00	0.00	0.00
3	0.09	0.07	0.03	0.20	0.18	0.08	0.00	0.00	0.00
4	0.11	0.09	0.05	0.25	0.22	0.10	0.01	0.01	0.00
5	0.14	0.11	0.06	0.30	0.26	0.13	0.01	0.01	0.00
6	0.15	0.11	0.07	0.34	0.29	0.16	0.02	0.02	0.01
7	0.15	0.10	0.08	0.37	0.32	0.18	0.04	0.03	0.02
8	0.15	0.10	0.08	0.40	0.34	0.20	0.06	0.04	0.03
9	0.14	0.09	0.08	0.43	0.36	0.22	0.07	0.05	0.05
10	0.13	0.09	0.08	0.45	0.37	0.23	0.09	0.06	0.06
11	0.13	0.09	0.07	0.47	0.39	0.25	0.10	0.07	0.07
12							0.11	0.07	0.07
13							0.12	0.08	0.08
14							0.13	0.08	0.09
15							0.14	0.09	0.09
16							0.14	0.09	0.10
17							0.15	0.10	0.11
18							0.16	0.11	0.11

NOTES: Sample restricted to Army enlistees.

Table 4.3
Mean Educational Outcomes, by Years Since Application: Army Non-Enlistees

Years Since Application	Current Enrollment			Cumulative Enrollment			Degree Attainment		
	All	2-Year	4-Year	All	2-Year	4-Year	All	2-Year	4-Year
0	0.11	0.09	0.05	0.11	0.09	0.05			
1	0.18	0.14	0.09	0.23	0.18	0.10			
2	0.19	0.15	0.09	0.28	0.23	0.13	0.01	0.01	0.00
3	0.18	0.13	0.10	0.31	0.26	0.15	0.02	0.01	0.01
4	0.17	0.12	0.10	0.34	0.28	0.16	0.03	0.02	0.02
5	0.15	0.10	0.09	0.36	0.30	0.18	0.05	0.04	0.04
6	0.13	0.09	0.08	0.38	0.32	0.19	0.07	0.05	0.05
7	0.12	0.08	0.07	0.40	0.33	0.20	0.09	0.06	0.07
8	0.10	0.07	0.06	0.41	0.34	0.21	0.11	0.06	0.08
9	0.09	0.06	0.05	0.42	0.35	0.22	0.12	0.07	0.09
10	0.08	0.05	0.05	0.42	0.35	0.23	0.13	0.08	0.10
11	0.08	0.05	0.05	0.42	0.35	0.23	0.13	0.08	0.11
12							0.14	0.09	0.11
13							0.15	0.09	0.11
14							0.15	0.09	0.12
15							0.16	0.10	0.12
16							0.16	0.10	0.12
17							0.17	0.11	0.13
18							0.17	0.11	0.12

NOTES: Sample restricted to applicants to the Army who never enlist.

Results

We report the results of estimating Equation 4.1 in two sections. The first section reports results for current and cumulative college enrollment, and the second section reports results for college degree attainment. In both sections, we report estimates by AFQT category, race/ethnicity, and two- versus four-year college outcomes.

College Enrollment

Figure 4.2 graphs the estimated effect of Army enlistment on current college enrollment by years since application for the 1998–2000 applicant cohorts.[1] In the first year following enlistment, our estimates imply that Army enlistment lowers the probability of current enrollment by 13 percentage points. However, the negative effect of enlistment on current enrollment diminishes with years since application. By the fifth year following application, our estimates

[1] We observe up to 11 years of enrollment data for this cohort (1998–2009). Enrollment data for the first nine years since application cover all applicant cohorts. For the tenth year since application, the data cover the 1999–2000 cohorts and, for the 11th year since application, the data cover the 2000 cohort only.

Figure 4.2
Estimated Effect of Army Enlistment on Current College Enrollment, by Years Since Application

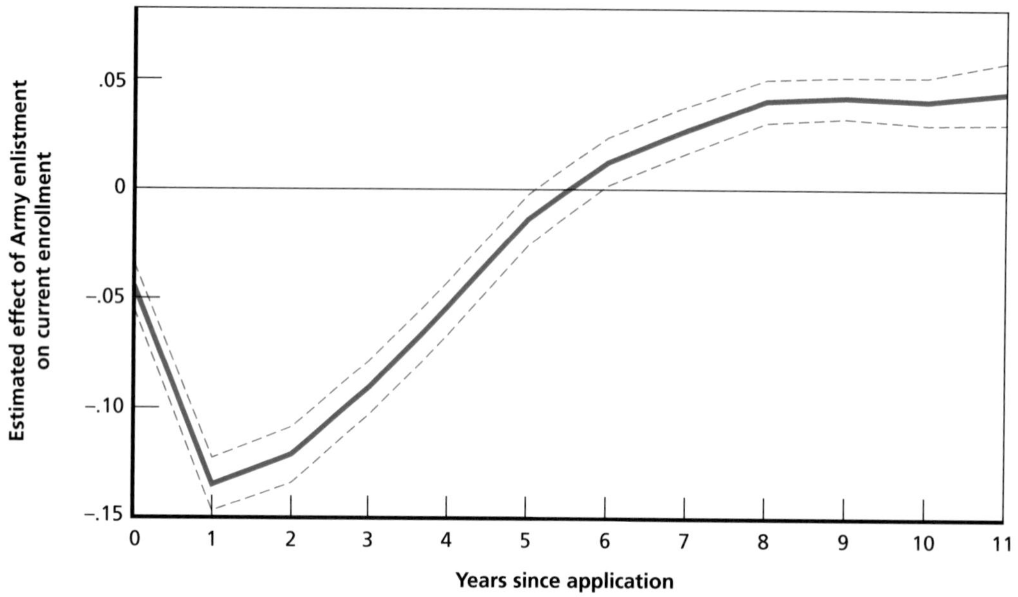

NOTES: Sample restricted to 1998–2000 Army applicant cohorts. Dashed lines denote 95 percent confidence intervals.
RAND *TR995-4.2*

imply that enlistment has no effect on current enrollment; 6–11 years following application, the estimates imply enlistment has a positive effect on current enrollment. These results are consistent with the hypothesis that enlistment delays college education.

Estimates for cumulative enrollment (Figure 4.3) tell a similar story. Enlistment lowers the likelihood of ever enrolling in college in the first seven years following application. However, by eight years following application, enlistment has no effect on cumulative enrollment. The estimates imply a 3.7 percentage point positive effect of enlistment on cumulative enrollment 11 years following application, suggesting that while enlistment delays college education, in the longer run, enlistment results in higher levels of college enrollment.

The estimates graphed in Figure 4.4 indicate that enlistment has a larger negative effect on cumulative enrollment for Category I and II enlistees than for Category III enlistees in the first few years following application. As a percentage of non-enlistee cumulative enrollment (which is considerably higher for Category I and II non-enlistees, see Table 4.3), however, the estimates imply similar effects across the three groups. In the longer run, the point estimates imply that enlistment has a positive effect on cumulative enrollment for all three groups, although only the estimate for Category IIIA enlistees is statistically significant in year 11.

Table 4.4 reports the estimated effect of Army enlistment on cumulative college enrollment by AFQT category and college type (two- versus four-year college). The overall pattern of estimated effects is similar across AFQT categories for two- and four-year college enrollments. In the longer run, the estimates suggest that enlistment might increase the likelihood of Category IIIA enrollment in two-year colleges. The statistically significant point estimate of six percentage points in year 11 represents an increase in two-year enrollment of about 15 percent over average non-enlistee two-year college enrollment rates (although this percentage effect is likely biased downward due to the downward bias in our measure of mean college enrollment).

Figure 4.3
Estimated Effect of Army Enlistment on Cumulative College Enrollment, by Years Since Application

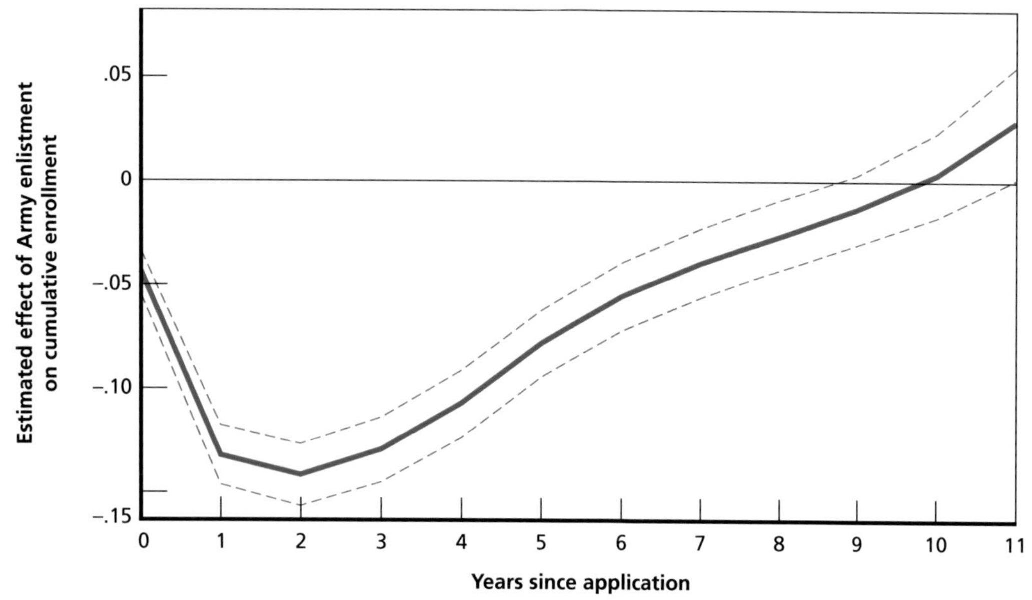

NOTES: Sample restricted to 1998–2000 Army applicant cohorts. Dashed lines denote 95 percent confidence intervals.
RAND *TR995-4.3*

Figure 4.4
Estimated Effect of Army Enlistment on Cumulative College Enrollment, by Years Since Application and AFQT Category

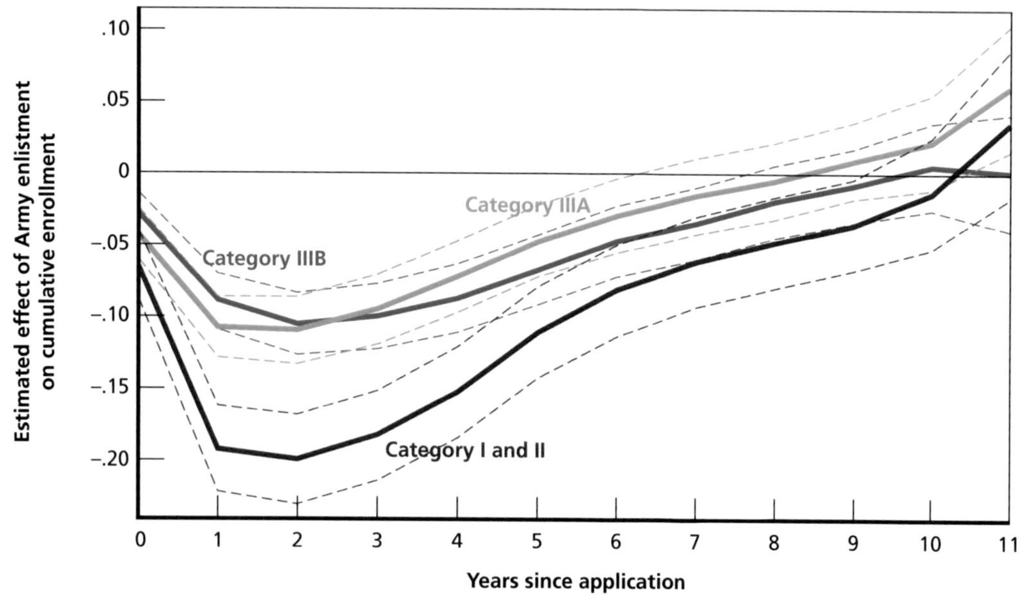

NOTES: Sample restricted to 1998–2000 Army applicant cohorts. Dashed lines denote 95 percent confidence intervals.
RAND *TR995-4.4*

Table 4.4
Estimated Effect of Army Enlistment on Cumulative Two- and Four-Year College Enrollment, by Years Since Application and AFQT Category

Years Since Application	2-Year			4-Year		
	Cats. I and II	Cat. IIIA	Cat. IIIB	Cats. I and II	Cat. IIIA	Cat. IIIB
0	–0.04	–0.03	–0.02	–0.03	–0.02	–0.01
1	–0.13	–0.08	–0.08	–0.12	–0.05	–0.03
2	–0.13	–0.09	–0.10	–0.13	–0.05	–0.03
3	–0.11	–0.08	–0.09	–0.13	–0.05	–0.04
4	–0.09	–0.06	–0.08	–0.12	–0.04	–0.03
5	–0.06	–0.03	–0.06	–0.10	–0.03	–0.02
6	–0.04	–0.02	–0.04	–0.07	–0.02	–0.02
7	–0.03	–0.01	–0.03	–0.06	–0.01	–0.01
8	–0.02	0.00	–0.02	–0.05	0.00	0.00
9	–0.01	0.01	–0.01	–0.04	0.02	0.01
10	0.00	0.02	0.00	–0.02	0.01	0.00
11	0.03	0.06	0.01	0.00	0.04	–0.01

NOTES: Sample restricted to 1998–2000 Army applicant cohorts.

Longer-run estimates for other AFQT categories are statistically indistinguishable from zero. Table 4.5 reveals no statistically significant difference in the estimated effect of enlistment on college enrollment across race/ethnicity categories.

College Degree Attainment

Figure 4.5 graphs the estimated effect of Army enlistment on the probability of earning a college degree by year since application for the 1991–1994 cohorts.[2] Consistent with the results for college enrollment, the college degree results imply that enlistment delays college education. Enlistment lowers the probability of completing a two-year college (four-year) degree by 2.3 (4.1) percentage points within seven years of application. The negative effect of enlistment decreases thereafter and becomes statistically indistinguishable from zero by 12 years following application for two-year degree attainment and 17 years following application for four-year degree attainment.

The fact that enlistment increases college enrollment, but not overall degree attainment, could imply that enlistees have lower college completion rates than civilians. However, the other possibility is that enrollment and degree attainment effects vary by application cohort, something that our data do not permit us to investigate directly.

As with college enrollment, our estimates imply that the negative effect of enlistment on college degree attainment in the short run is greatest for Category I and II enlistees (see Figures 4.6 and 4.7). This is unsurprising, since high-aptitude youth overall are more likely to attend college. In the longer run, 18 years following application, the point estimates suggest a negative effect of enlistment on college degree attainment for Category I and II and

[2] We observe up to 18 years of degree data for this cohort (1991–1994). Degree data for the first 16 years since application cover all applicant cohorts. For the 16th year since application, the data cover the 1992–1994 cohorts; for the 17th year since application, the data cover the 1993–1994 cohorts; and, for the 18th year since application, the data cover the 1994 cohort only.

Table 4.5
Estimated Effect of Army Enlistment on Cumulative Two- and Four-Year College Enrollment, by Years Since Application and Race/Ethnicity

Years Since Application	2-Year			4-Year		
	White	Black	Hispanic	White	Black	Hispanic
0	−0.03	−0.03	−0.04	−0.01	−0.02	−0.03
1	−0.09	−0.11	−0.10	−0.05	−0.10	−0.06
2	−0.10	−0.11	−0.12	−0.06	−0.10	−0.06
3	−0.09	−0.10	−0.09	−0.06	−0.11	−0.06
4	−0.07	−0.09	−0.07	−0.05	−0.10	−0.06
5	−0.05	−0.07	−0.04	−0.04	−0.10	−0.05
6	−0.04	−0.05	−0.02	−0.02	−0.09	−0.04
7	−0.02	−0.04	−0.01	−0.01	−0.08	−0.03
8	−0.01	−0.03	0.00	0.00	−0.07	−0.02
9	0.00	−0.02	0.01	0.01	−0.05	0.00
10	0.01	−0.02	0.03	0.02	−0.07	−0.01
11	0.04	0.01	0.03	0.03	−0.06	0.00

Notes: Sample restricted to 1998–2000 Army applicant cohorts.

Figure 4.5
Estimated Effect of Army Enlistment on College Degree Attainment, by Years Since Application

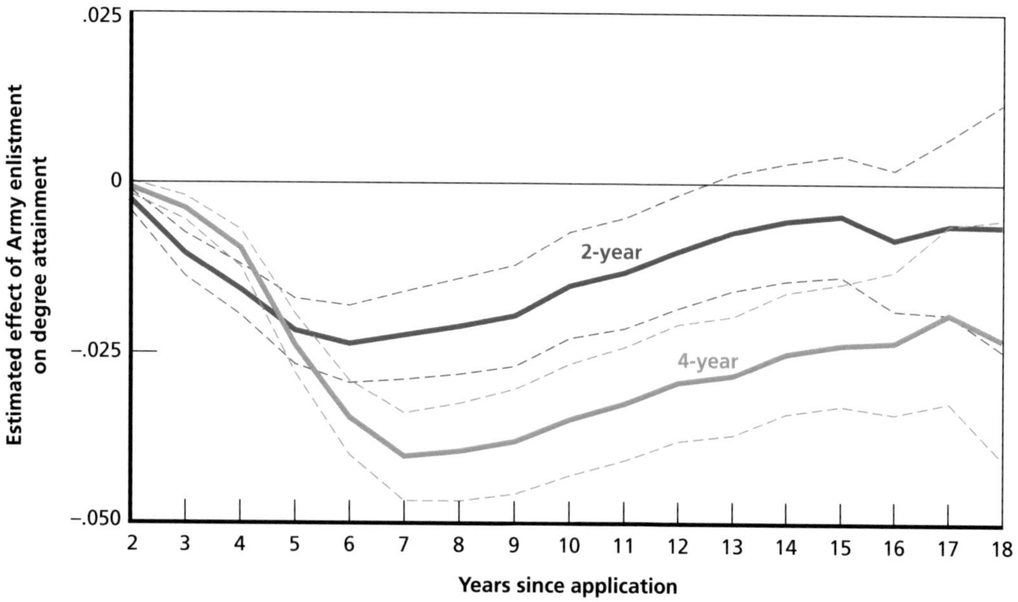

NOTES: Sample restricted to 1991–1994 Army applicant cohorts. Dashed lines denote 95 percent confidence intervals.
RAND *TR995-4.5*

Category IIIA youth and a positive effect on college degree attainment of Category IIIB youth. None of these estimates, however, are statistically significant. Figure 4.8 shows a statistically significant positive effect of enlistment on two-year degree attainment among African Americans. The effect of Army enlistment on four-year degree attainment (Figure 4.9) is not statistically significant for any race/ethnicity category.

Figure 4.6
Estimated Effect of Army Enlistment on Two-Year College Degree Attainment, by Years Since Application and AFQT Category

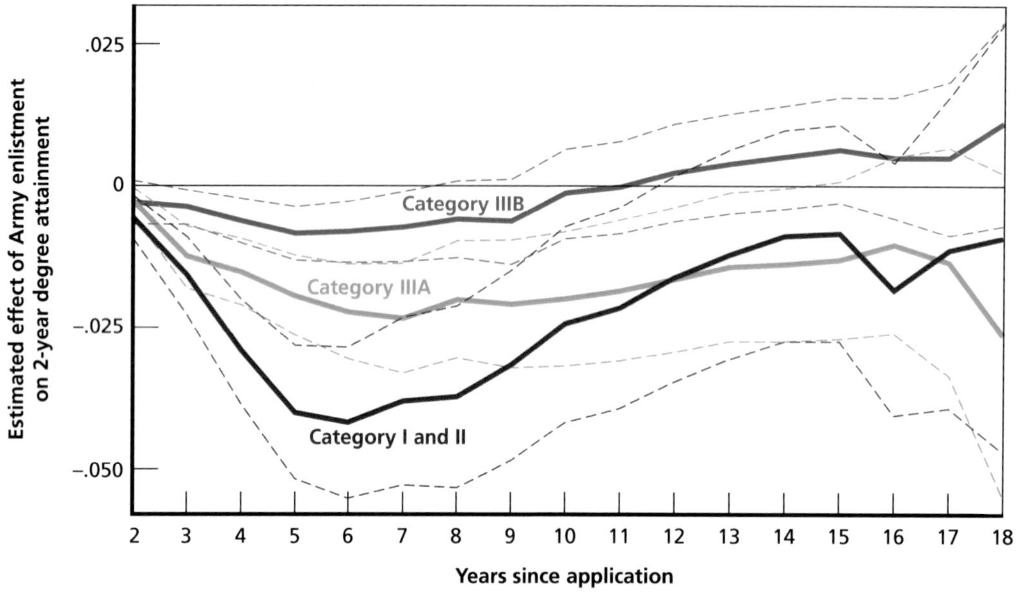

NOTES: Sample restricted to 1991–1994 Army applicant cohorts. Dashed lines denote 95 percent confidence intervals.

RAND *TR995-4.6*

Figure 4.7
Estimated Effect of Army Enlistment on Four-Year College Degree Attainment, by Years Since Application and AFQT Category

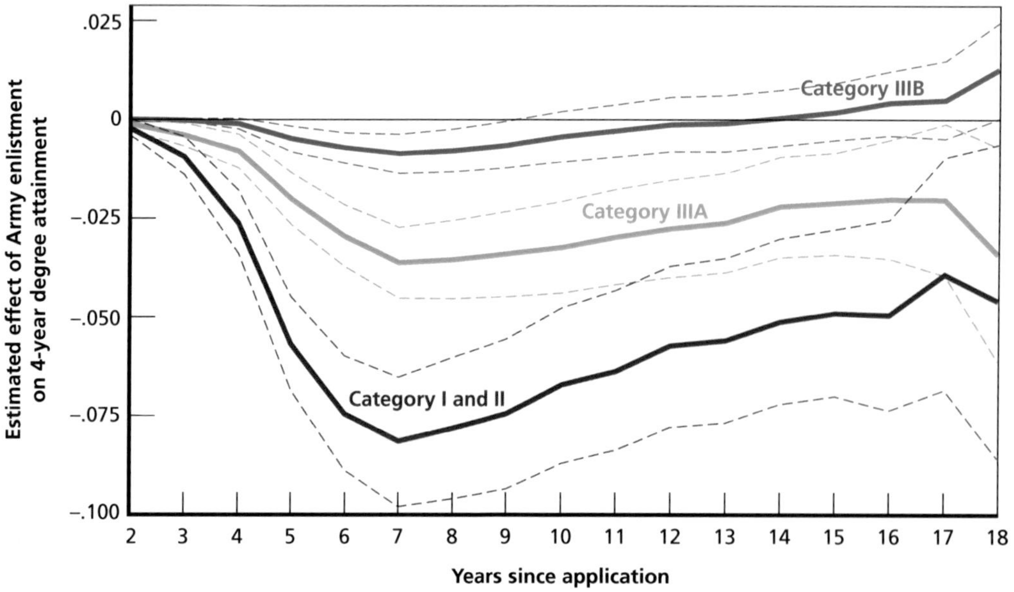

NOTES: Sample restricted to 1991–1994 Army applicant cohorts. Dashed lines denote 95 percent confidence intervals.

RAND *TR995-4.7*

Figure 4.8
Estimated Effect of Army Enlistment on Two-Year College Degree Attainment, by Years Since Application and Race/Ethnicity

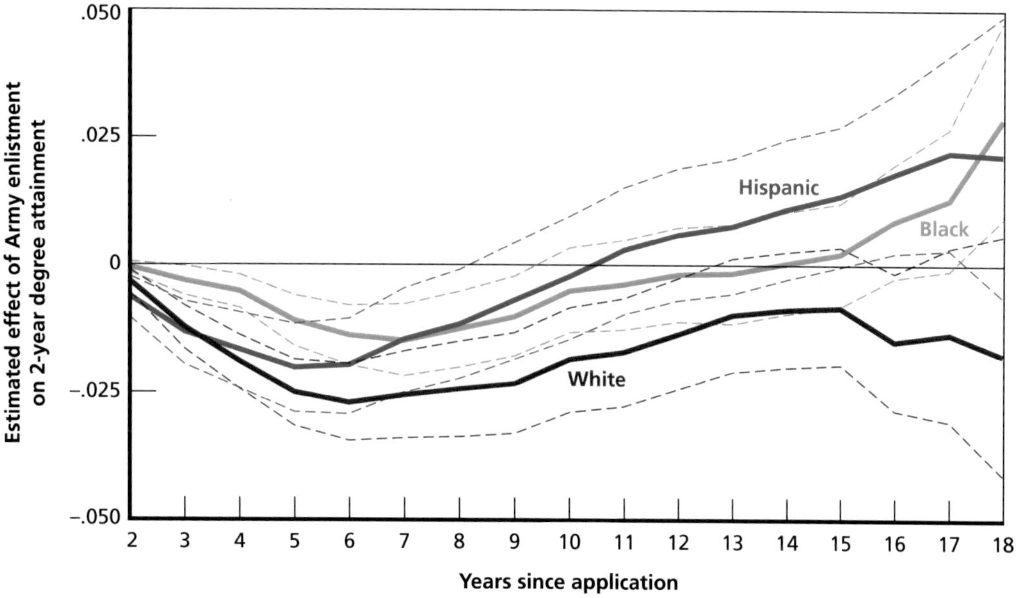

NOTES: Sample restricted to 1991–1994 Army applicant cohorts. Dashed lines denote 95 percent confidence intervals.
RAND *TR995-4.8*

Figure 4.9
Estimated Effect of Army Enlistment on Four-Year College Degree Attainment, by Years Since Application and Race/Ethnicity

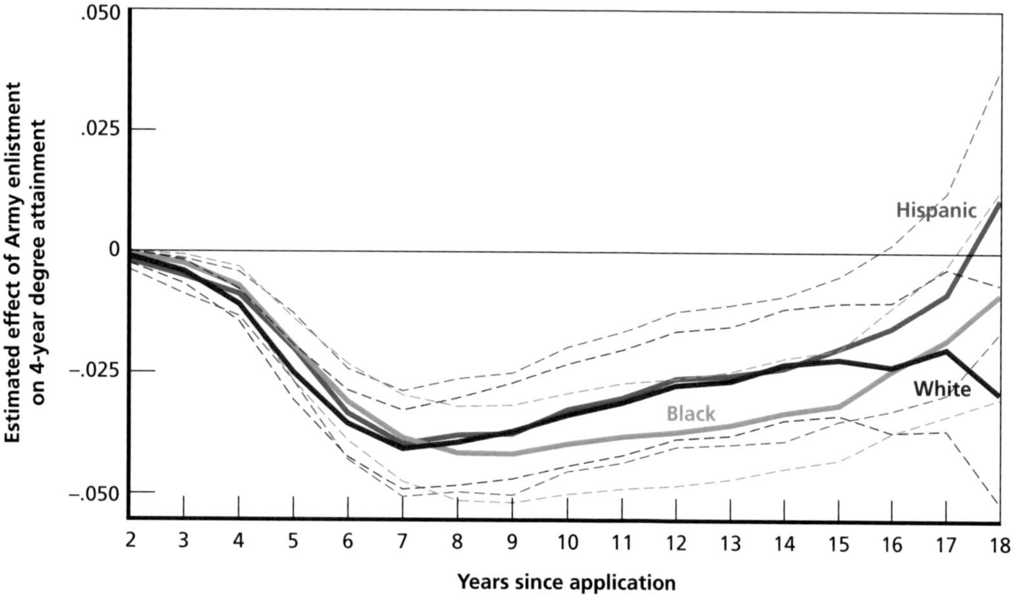

NOTES: Sample restricted to 1991–1994 Army applicant cohorts. Dashed lines denote 95 percent confidence intervals.
RAND *TR995-4.9*

Summary

The education estimates reported above clearly indicate that Army enlistment delays college education. The longer-run effects of Army enlistment on college enrollment and degree attainment are much less clear, due to the relatively large standard errors surrounding those estimates.

Figure 4.10 graphs estimates of the effect of enlistment on two- and four-year college degree attainment for all services combined, for which we have larger samples. These estimates also are not particularly precise, but do nonetheless suggest that enlistment has the effect of increasing two-year college degree attainment while decreasing four-year degree attainment. Looking at estimates by AFQT category (Figures 4.11 and 4.12) further suggests that the negative four-year degree effect is accounted for by Category I and II enlistees. Enlistment appears to increase two-year degree attainment among all three AFQT category enlistees.

Figure 4.10
Estimated Effect of Enlistment on College Degree Attainment, by Years Since Application: All Services Combined

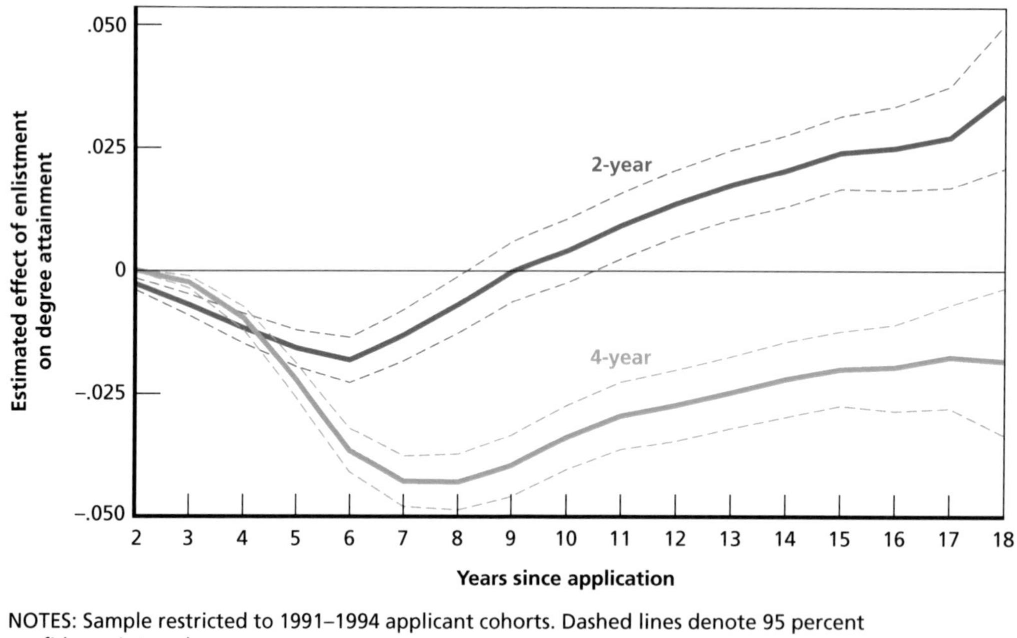

NOTES: Sample restricted to 1991–1994 applicant cohorts. Dashed lines denote 95 percent confidence intervals.
RAND *TR995-4.10*

Figure 4.11
Estimated Effect of Enlistment on Two-Year College Degree Attainment, by Years Since Application and AFQT Category: All Services Combined

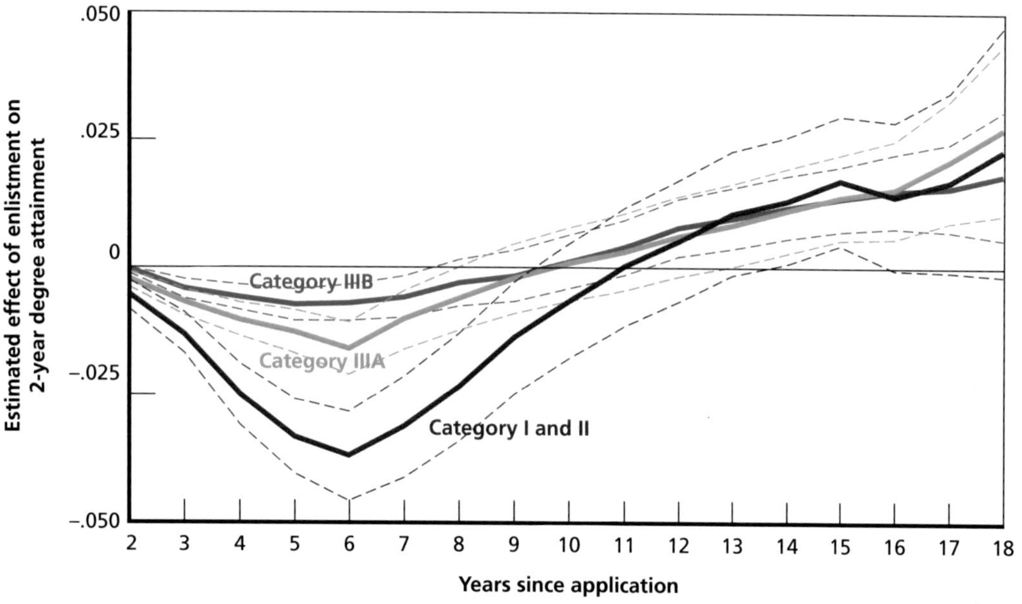

NOTES: Sample restricted to 1991–1994 applicant cohorts. Dashed lines denote 95 percent confidence intervals.

RAND *TR995-4.11*

Figure 4.12
Estimated Effect of Enlistment on Four-Year College Degree Attainment, by Years Since Application and AFQT Category: All Services Combined

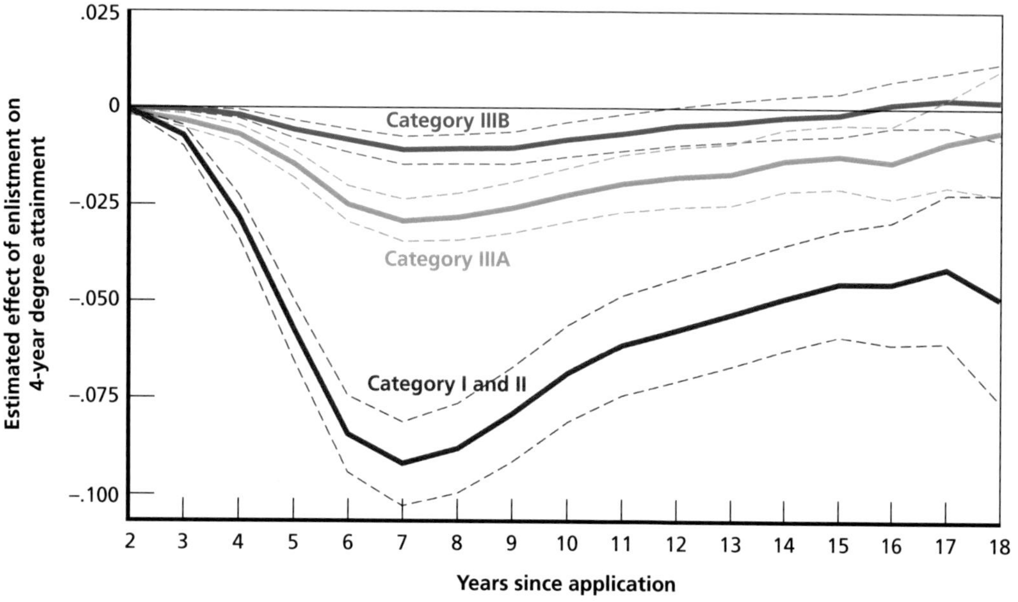

NOTES: Sample restricted to 1991–1994 applicant cohorts. Dashed lines denote 95 percent confidence intervals.

RAND *TR995-4.12*

CHAPTER FIVE

Conclusion

This research has sought to estimate the causal effect of military enlistment on labor market earnings and educational attainment. In the All-Volunteer era, making such an estimate is complicated by the fact that military service is highly selective: Individuals volunteer for military service, and the military chooses among those volunteers on the basis of a wide range of criteria that are themselves correlated with earnings and education. To mitigate the bias this type of selection can impart to empirical estimates, we restricted our analysis to qualified military applicants, controlling for a wide-range of applicant characteristics.

Our estimates imply that enlistment has a strong, positive effect on earnings in the first few years following application, when the vast majority of enlistees are still serving in the active component. The average effect of Army enlistment across our 15 applicant cohorts two years following application amounts to 42 percent of annual non-enlistee earnings. The positive effect of enlistment, however, diminishes during the period in which large numbers of enlistees separate from the active component. During these years, our education estimates imply that significant numbers of these enlistees are attending college and so are most likely not working in civilian employment full-time. As these enlistees complete their college education and begin civilian careers in earnest, the effect of enlistment on earnings begins to grow again. In the longer-run, between 14 and 18 years following application, our estimates imply that Army enlistment increases annual earnings by 11 percent.

The short-run earnings effects we estimate are unsurprising, since the alternative to military service for many young men and women is college rather than full-time work. In addition, it could very well be that the military must offer a relatively high wage in order to induce individuals to choose enlistment and the risks and hardships it entails. That enlistment might convey longer-run benefits in the labor market is perhaps of greater significance for military manpower policy.

There are at least three potential explanations for these longer-run, positive earnings effects. First, it could be that enlistment induces enlistees to obtain more formal education than they otherwise would have and that this greater educational attainment has returns in the labor market. We find, at best, weak evidence in support of this hypothesis. On the one hand, our estimates clearly indicate that enlistment causes enlistees to delay their college education. All else equal, we might expect such a delay to depress longer-run labor market earnings. However, our estimates also indicate that enlistment increases the likelihood that enlistees will obtain a two-year college degree, although these estimates are statistically significant only when looking at all services combined. The increase in two-year degree attainment does not emerge until 16–18 years following enlistment, and the value of obtaining such a degree at that age might be much less than at some earlier age. Moreover, for Category I and II enlistees, the evidence suggests that the increase in two-year degree attainment comes at the expense of a decrease in four-year degree attainment. Thus, the overall effect of enlistment on two-year college degree attainment is small in both absolute and relative terms, and together with the results for four-year degrees suggests that it is unlikely that education effects could account for the substantial longer-run earnings effects we estimate.

If enlistment does not have a strong effect on educational attainment, then what explains the longer-run earnings effects we observe? Two possibilities are that (1) military service develops other skills that are valued in the labor market and (2) the military pays above-average wages in order to compensate individuals for their sacrifice and service (a "compensating wage differential"). We do not directly test these alternative hypotheses, but we do find that the positive effect of enlistment on longer-run earnings is concentrated among enlistees who are still serving in the active component. The earnings of Category IIIA and IIIB Army enlistees still serving in the military between 14 and 18 years following enlistment are 125 and 155 percent higher, respectively, than the earnings of comparable non-enlistees. By contrast, Category IIIA and IIIB Army enlistees who have separated by 14–18 years following enlistment earn 3 and 6 percent more than comparable non-enlistees, respectively. Category I and II Army enlistees still serving at that juncture earn 84 percent more than comparable non-enlistees, but those enlistees who have separated earn 6 percent less.

The magnitude of the differences in earnings estimates in later years between enlistees who do and do not continue to serve suggests that some of the longer-run earnings effects are attributable to a compensating wage differential. For Category I and II enlistees, it seems likely that this differential explains all of the positive longer-run earnings gains observed for that group as a whole, since the correlation between enlistment and earnings of those who have separated from active-component service is actually negative and our estimates further suggest that enlistment could cause Category I and II enlistees to obtain less formal education than they otherwise would have. Category IIIA and IIIB enlistees, on the other hand, appear to benefit from enlistment even after they separate, although their earnings gains are fairly modest. This suggests that military service may, in fact, help at least some individuals develop skills that convey longer-run benefits in the civilian labor market.

In the All-Volunteer era, the overriding objective of compensation policy is to attract and retain the force necessary to meet the nation's national security objectives. If individuals believe they will be well served by this experience, more might be willing to enlist. Furthermore, from a societal perspective, the electorate might be more willing to support putting young men and women at risk for the sake of national defense if it believes these individuals will benefit financially. The estimates reported in this document suggest that, for the bulk of the enlisted force, military service provides tangible benefits in terms of longer-term earnings. On average, these individuals will earn more and obtain as much, or more, formal education as they otherwise would have. The evidence for the highest-aptitude youth is mixed. Clearly, in the short run, these individuals experience substantial earnings gains as a result of military service. However, those earnings gains erode over time and, for those who do not remain in the military, eventually turn slightly negative, perhaps because enlistment delays college and permanently lowers the likelihood they will obtain a four-year college degree.

The Effect of Enlistment on Labor Market Earnings: All Services

Table A.1
Estimated Effect of Enlistment on Earnings ($2005, thousands), by Years Since Application and Service: All Applicant Cohorts

Years Since Application	Army		Air Force		Navy		Marine Corps	
	Mean	Percentage	Mean	Percentage	Mean	Percentage	Mean	Percentage
0	0.6	13	0.4	7	0.5	12	0.3	7
1	3.0	40	2.8	33	2.5	36	1.9	26
2	4.3	42	4.4	38	4.4	46	3.5	33
3	4.6	35	5.3	36	5.5	44	4.4	32
4	4.2	26	6.0	33	6.4	40	4.5	26
5	3.5	18	5.3	24	5.8	30	2.7	14
6	2.9	14	4.6	19	4.5	21	1.8	8
7	2.6	11	3.9	15	3.7	16	2.0	8
8	2.4	10	3.8	14	3.3	13	2.2	8
9	2.3	9	4.1	14	3.1	12	2.2	8
10	2.3	8	4.2	14	3.4	12	2.3	8
11	2.4	8	4.4	14	3.7	12	2.5	8
12	2.6	8	4.4	13	3.6	12	2.5	8
13	2.8	9	4.8	14	3.8	12	2.5	7
14	3.3	10	5.3	15	4.0	12	2.5	7
15	4.0	12	6.7	18	4.6	14	2.8	8
16	4.1	12	7.0	18	4.7	14	3.1	9
17	3.6	10	5.8	15	4.1	12	2.4	6
18	3.0	9	6.3	16	3.4	10	1.9	5

NOTES: Earnings ($2005) include allowances and bonuses. Earnings effect is a weighted average of earnings effects over all applicant cohorts. Percentage earnings effect is relative to average non-enlistee earnings.

Table A.2
Estimated Effect of Enlistment on Earnings ($2005, thousands), by Years Since Application and Year of Application: All Services Combined

Years Since Application	Application Year															
	1989	1990	1991	1992	1993	1994	1995	1996	1997	1998	1999	2000	2001	2002	2003	Avg.
0						0.5	0.4	0.4	0.3	0.3	0.7	0.7	1.4	1.5	3.9	0.5
1					3.4	2.7	3.0	2.6	2.6	2.8	3.6	4.1	7.7	5.9	6.2	2.6
2				5.1	4.8	4.4	4.2	4.1	4.2	4.6	5.4	7.8	10.6	7.9	4.5	4.2
3			4.9	4.6	4.5	3.8	4.2	4.1	4.4	5.8	8.3	9.8	11.2	8.1	4.4	5.0
4		4.2	3.6	3.8	3.2	3.0	3.6	4.3	5.3	8.2	9.8	9.7	10.9	7.7	2.2	5.2
5	2.2	2.4	2.2	2.1	1.9	1.8	2.7	3.7	5.8	7.9	7.8	8.1	8.4	6.0		4.3
6	1.3	1.6	1.2	1.3	1.3	1.3	2.5	4.3	5.7	6.7	7.1	6.7	7.1			3.5
7	0.9	1.1	0.9	0.9	1.3	1.5	3.2	4.9	5.6	6.8	6.2	6.2				3.0
8	0.5	0.7	0.7	0.8	1.6	2.3	4.0	5.3	6.2	6.5	6.1					2.9
9	0.0	0.5	1.1	1.2	2.6	3.2	4.4	5.7	5.8	6.5						2.8
10	0.1	0.8	1.7	2.4	3.4	3.5	5.0	5.6	5.9							2.9
11	0.4	1.3	2.7	3.3	3.7	4.0	5.2	6.1								3.1
12	0.7	2.0	3.3	3.6	4.3	4.1	5.7									3.2
13	1.5	2.8	3.8	4.1	4.5	4.4										3.4
14	2.2	3.3	4.5	4.3	4.9											3.7
15	3.4	4.4	5.3	5.1												4.5
16	3.8	4.6	5.6													4.6
17	3.4	4.6														3.9
18	3.5															3.5

NOTES: Earnings ($2005) include allowances and bonuses. Average treatment effect is weighted by number of enlistees in each application year.

Table A.3
Estimated Effect of Enlistment on Earnings ($2005, thousands), by Years Since Application and AFQT Category: All Services and Applicant Cohorts Combined

Years Since Application	Categories I and II		Category IIIA		Category IIIB	
	Mean	Percentage	Mean	Percentage	Mean	Percentage
0	0.4	9	0.5	12	0.5	12
1	2.6	33	2.7	38	2.6	37
2	4.3	39	4.1	40	4.2	42
3	5.1	36	4.9	37	4.8	38
4	5.4	30	5.1	32	5.0	33
5	4.2	20	4.3	22	4.4	24
6	2.8	12	3.6	17	4.2	22
7	1.9	7	3.3	15	4.3	21
8	1.6	6	3.3	14	4.2	19
9	1.6	5	3.2	13	4.1	18
10	1.6	5	3.5	13	4.3	17
11	1.8	5	3.6	13	4.5	18
12	1.8	5	3.7	13	4.6	18
13	1.9	5	4.2	14	4.9	18
14	2.1	5	4.6	15	5.3	20
15	2.7	7	5.2	17	6.3	23
16	2.9	7	5.4	17	6.4	23
17	2.0	5	4.6	14	6.0	21
18	1.1	2	4.4	13	5.8	20

NOTES: Earnings ($2005) include allowances and bonuses. Earnings effect is a weighted average of earnings effects over all applicant cohorts. Percentage earnings effect is relative to average non-enlistee earnings.

References

Angrist, Joshua D., "Lifetime Earnings and the Vietnam Era Draft Lottery: Evidence from Social Security Administrative Records," *American Economic Review*, Vol. 80, No. 3, June 1990, pp. 313–336.

———, "Estimating the Labor Market Impact of Voluntary Military Service Using Social Security Data on Military Applicants," *Econometrica,* Vol. 66, No. 2, March 1998, pp. 249–288.

Angrist, Joshua D., and Stacey H. Chen, *Long-Term Effect of Vietnam-Era Conscription: Schooling, Experience and Earnings*, Cambridge, Mass.: National Bureau of Economic Research (NBER), WP-13411, September 2007.

Angrist, Joshua D., and Alan B. Krueger, "Why Do World War II Veterans Earn More Than Nonveterans?" *Journal of Labor Economics*, Vol. 12, No. 1, January 1994, pp. 74–97.

Asch, Beth J., James R. Hosek, and Craig W. Martin, *A Look at Cash Compensation for Active Duty Military Personnel*, Santa Monica, Calif.: RAND Corporation, MR-1492-OSD, 2002. As of June 27, 2011: http://www.rand.org/pubs/monograph_reports/MR1492.html

Asch, Beth J., and John T. Warner, *An Examination of the Effects of Voluntary Separation Incentives*, Santa Monica, Calif.: RAND Corporation, MR-859-OSD, 2001. As of June 27, 2011: http://www.rand.org/pubs/monograph_reports/MR859.html

Bryant, Richard R., V. A. Samaranayake, and Allen Wilhite, "The Effect of Military Service on the Subsequent Civilian Wage of the Post-Vietnam Veteran," *Quarterly Review of Economics and Finance*, Vol. 74, 1993, pp. 15–30.

Daymont, Thomas, and Paul J. Andrisani, *Academic Returns to Military Service*, Fort Knox, Ky: U.S. Department of the Army, U.S. Army Recruiting Command, 1998.

Furstenberg Jr., Frank F., Ruben G. Rumbaut, and Richard A. Settersten Jr., "On the Frontier of Adulthood: Emerging Themes and New Directions," in Frank F. Furstenberg Jr., Ruben G. Rumbaut, and Richard A. Settersten Jr., eds., *On the Frontier of Adulthood: Theory, Research, and Public Policy*, London: University of Chicago Press, 2005.

Goldberg, Matthew S., and John T. Warner, "Military Experience, Civilian Experience, and the Earnings of Veterans," *Journal of Human Resources*, Vol. 22, No. 1, Winter 1987, pp. 62–81.

Grissmer, David W., *Impact of the Military Drawdown on Youth Employment, Training, and Educational Opportunity*, Santa Monica, Calif.: RAND Corporation, P-7734, 1992. As of June 27, 2011: http://www.rand.org/pubs/papers/P7734.html

Hirsch, Barry T., and Stephen L. Mehay, "Evaluating the Labor Market Performance of Veterans Using a Matched Comparison Group Design," *Journal of Human Resources*, Vol. 38, No. 3, Summer 2003, pp. 673–700.

Hosek, James, and Paco Martorell, *How Have Deployments During the War on Terrorism Affected Reenlistment?* Santa Monica, Calif.: RAND Corporation, MG-873-OSD, 2009. As of July 15, 2011: http://www.rand.org/pubs/monographs/MG873

Hosek, James R., and Michael G. Mattock, *Learning About Quality: How the Quality of Military Personnel Is Revealed Over Time*, Santa Monica, Calif.: RAND Corporation, MR-1593-OSD, 2003. As of June 28, 2011: http://www.rand.org/pubs/monograph_reports/MR1593.html

Hosek, James R., Michael G. Mattock, Michael Schoenbaum, and Elizabeth Eiseman, *Placing a Value on the Health Care Benefit for Active-Duty Personnel*, Santa Monica, Calif.: RAND Corporation, MG-385-OSD, 2005. As of June 27, 2011:
http://www.rand.org/pubs/monographs/MG385.html

Kelty, Ryan, Meredith Kleykamp, and David Segal, "The Military and the Transition to Adulthood," *Transition to Adulthood*, Vol. 20, No. 1, Spring 2010, pp. 181–207.

Krueger, Alan B. , "Inequality, Too Much of a Good Thing," in James J. Heckman, Alan B. Krueger, and Benjamin Friedman, eds., *Inequality in America: What Role for Human Capital Policies?* Cambridge, Mass.: MIT Press, 2004, pp. 1–77.

Magnum, Stephen L., and David E. Ball, "The Transferability of Military-Provided Occupational Training in the Post-Draft Era," *Industrial and Labor Relations Review*, Vol. 42, No. 2, January 1989, pp. 230–245.

Neal, Derek A., and William R. Johnson, "The Role of Premarket Factors in Black-White Wage Differences," *Journal of Political Economy*, Vol. 104, No. 5, October 1996, pp. 869–895.

Office of the Secretary of Defense, "Regular Military Compensation Calculator," no date. As of June 28, 2011:
http://militarypay.defense.gov/mpcalcs/Calculators/RMC.aspx

Office of the Under Secretary of Defense for Personnel and Readiness, *Report of the Tenth Quadrennial Review of Military Compensation,* Volume 1, *Cash Compensation*, Washington, D.C.: U.S. Department of Defense, February 2008.

———, *Population Representation in the Military Services: Fiscal Year 2009 Report*, Washington, D.C.: U.S. Department of Defense, 2010. As of June 28, 2011:
http://prhome.defense.gov/mpp/ACCESSION%20POLICY/PopRep2009/download/download.html

OUSD P&R—*See* Office of the Under Secretary of Defense for Personnel and Readiness.

Phillips, Robert, Phillip Andrisani, Thomas Daymont, and Curtis Gilroy, "The Economic Returns to Military Service: Race-Ethnic Differences," *Social Science Quarterly*, Vol. 73, No. 2, June 1992, pp. 340–359.

Simon, Curtis J., Sebastian Negrusa, and John T. Warner, "Educational Benefits and Military Service: An Analysis of Enlistment, Reenlistment, and Veterans' Benefit Usage 1991–2005," *Economic Inquiry*, Vol. 48, No. 4, October 2010, pp. 1008–1031.

Social Security Administration, "Code of Federal Regulations, Title 20, Part 404: Federal Old-Age, Survivors and Disability Insurance (1950–)," web page, 2011. As of June 28, 2011:
http://www.ssa.gov/OP_Home/cfr20/404/404-0000.htm

Stafford, Frank P., "Partial Careers: Civilian Earnings and the Optimal Duration of an Army Career," in Curtis Gilroy, D. Horne, and D. Smith, eds., *Military Compensation Policies and Personnel Retention: Models and Evidence*, Alexandria, Va.: U.S. Army Research Institute for the Behavioral and Social Sciences, 1991, pp. 281–307.

Symonds, William C., Robert B. Schwartz, and Ronald Ferguson, *Pathways to Prosperity: Meeting the Challenge of Preparing Young Americans for the 21st Century*, report issued by the Pathways to Prosperity Project, Cambridge, Mass.: Harvard Graduate School of Education, February 2011.

U.S. Department of Defense, *Ninth Quadrennial Review of Military Compensation*, Washington, D.C., 2002. As of June 28, 2011:
http://prhome.defense.gov/MPP/qrmc/index.htm